Dairy-Free, Egg-Free Kid Pleasing Recipes & Tips

A comprehensive cookbook for parents of children with dairy, egg, and nut allergies, including 42 Super Quick Meals for Tired Mothers

by
Theresa Kingma

TABLE OF CONTENTS

Introduction 7

Dinners with Chicken
Chicken Curry 10
Chicken Nuggets 11
BBQ Chicken Pie 12
Slow Cook Chicken Drumsticks 13
Mandarin Chicken 14
Chicken Casablanca 15
Chicken Cacciatore 16
Chicken Enchiladas 17
Roasted Chicken 18
Easy Crock Pot Chicken 19
Stir Fry Chicken 20
Chicken Lemon Sauté 21
Chicken and Rice Casserole 22
Chicken Shish Kebabs 23
Mu Shu Chicken Wraps 24
Teriyaki Chicken Kebabs 25
Tarragon Chicken Bun Boats 26
Chicken Mole 27
Chicken Pot Pie 28
Chicken Paprikash Potatoes 30
Crock Pot Chicken Cassoulet 31
Chicken Strips 32

Dinners with Beef
Beef Curry 33
Slow Cooker Beef Goulash 34
Empanadas 35
Beef and Broccoli 36
Slow Cooked Chili 37
Pot Roast 38
Chili Mac 39
Spaghetti 40
Jambalaya 41
Swedish Meatballs 42
Meatloaf 43
Tamale Pie 44
Chile Verde 45
Slow Cooker Beef Stew 46
Shepherd's Pie 47
Flank Steak 48
Korean Barbecued Beef Strips 49
Hamburger Gravy 50
One-Pot Beef and Rice 51

Dinners with Pork

Creamed Pork on Toast Points 52
Slow Cook Pork Ribs 53
Baked Ham 53
Scalloped Potatoes with Ham 54
Bacon Pasties 55
Honey Mustard Pork Chops 56
Chili Verde 57

Dinners with Seafood

Shrimp and Pasta 58
Poached Salmon 59
Shrimp Cocktail. 59
Barbequed Salmon 60
Pan Fried Trout 61
Crab Legs 61
Creamy Tuna Vegetable Noodle 62
Shrimp Shish Kebabs 63
Teriyaki Shrimp/Scallop Kebabs. . . . 64
Easy Oven Fish 65

Dinners with Tofu

Tofu Stir-Fry 66
Tofu Indonesian-Style 67
Tofu Spaghetti 68

Miscellaneous Main Meals

Slow Cooked Beans 69
Smokey Roll Ups 70
Kingma Korn Puppies 71
Pizza 72
Pancakes 74
Waffles 75
Fettuccini Alfredo 76
Breakfast Citrus Sauce 77
Special Occasion Apple Pancakes . . . 78

Super Quick Meals for Tired Mothers

42 menus 80

Vegan Meals

12 menus 87

Soups

Split Pea 89
Baked Potato Soup 90
Cream of Mushroom 91
Chicken Tortilla Soup 92
Chicken Confetti Soup 93
Quick Potato Soup 94

Side Dishes

"Aunt Jean's" Rice 95
Creamy Noodles 96
Turnip Sauté 96
Brown-Sugar Carrots 97
Honey Carrots 97
Broccoli Strudel 98
German Potato Salad 99
Sweet Potato Casserole 100
Crunchy Salad 101
Spanish Rice 102
Corn-on-the-Cob Delight 103

Muffins & Breads

Orangey Rolls 104
Chocolate Babka 105
Streusel Raspberry Dessert Bread . . . 107
Scones with Streusel Topping 108
Blueberry Muffins 109
Apple Muffins with Streusel Topping . . . 110
S'more Muffins 111
Jelly-Filled Muffins 112
Pumpkin Muffins 113
Chocolate Pretzels 114
Sweet Pretzels 115
Biscuits 116
Sweet Potato Biscuits 117
Sweet Corn Bread 118
Banana Bread 119
Zucchini Bread 120
Focaccia Bread 121
Marvelous Monkey Bread 122

Desserts
Cookies

Oatmeal Cranberry Cookies 123
Glazed Raspberry Crunch Cookies . . . 124
Chocolate Chip Cookies, Kingma Style . . . 125
Button Cookies 126
Elephant Ears 127
Cranberry Cookies with Coconut . . . 128
Bee My Honey Cookies 129
Orangey Coconut Cookies 130
Gingerbread People Cookies 131
Snickerdoodles 132
Candy Cane Cookies 133
Sugar Cookies 134
Santa's Whiskers 135
Chocolate Sandwich Cookies 136
Eli's Chocolate Marshmallow Cookies . . . 137

Grandma's No Bake Cookies 138

Cakes
Easy Chocolate Cake 139
Special Snack Cake 140
Streusel Coffee Cake 142
Rhubarb Cake 143
Lemon Pound Cake 144
Upside-Down Fudge Cake 145
Chocolate Banana Cake Bars 146
Kingma's Favorite Chocolate Cupcakes . . . 147
Pineapple Upside Down Cake 148
White Cake 149
Heirloom Applesauce Cake 150

Goodies
Chocolate Pudding 151
Raspberry Shortbread Bars 152
Tasty Pumpkin Bars 153
Brownies 154
Crispy Rice Goodies 155
Homemade Popsicles 155
Yogurt Cups 156
Fruit Smoothies. 157
Easy Holiday Dairy-free Fudge 157
Popcorn Balls 158
Blackberry Pie 159
Peach Cobbler 160
Apple Crisp 161
Spider Web Chocolates 162
"Halleluiah, It's Ice Cream Time!" Soy Ice Cream . 163
Chocolate Chunks 164
Pumpkin Pie Tarts 165
Oatmeal Jelly Bars 166

Snacks
Tons of Snack Ideas 167
Pepperoni Roll Ups 169
Meat Roll Ups 169
Fun Time Granola Bars 170
"Even Healthier" Granola Bars 171
Seasoned Cereal Snack Mix 172
Quesadillas 172
Hummus 173
Eggplant Dip 174
Dairy-free, Nut-free Kid Pleasing Granola . . 175
Creamy Bean Dip for Chips . . . 176
Dairy-free, Egg-free Ranch Dip for Vegetables . . 176

Substitutions 177

Tips
Vitamins 179
Juice 179
Soy Milk 179
Snacks 180
Food Alternatives 180
Food Prep Ideas 181
Safe Places 182
Recommended Books and Support Systems . . 183
Warnings 185
Labeling and Contact information . . . 187
Party Planning 187
Weight Gain Ideas 189
Website Information 189
School 190

Final Thoughts 192

Introduction

"Get ready to call 9-1-1, it sounds like he is having an allergic reaction," the nurse warned me over the telephone. I frowned at my husband, who was holding our bright red, puffy, ten-month-old son Evan. His face that evening had suddenly swelled up and turned an alarming shade of red. I wracked my brain to figure out a cause for this response. And then I remembered the Chow Mein crunchy noodle he had sucked on earlier in the day.

Luckily, we didn't require an ambulance that night. But Evan's, and consequently our family's, dramatic and perilous journey with a life threatening food allergy began. So far, we have navigated through life without any potentially fatal mistakes. It was tough to make the transition into a dairy-free, egg-free, nut-free culinary routine, but we have settled into a comfortable life.

When you get lemons, make lemonade. This simple, trite cliché inspired the creation of this book. I wanted something positive to arise from our ordeal. From the overwhelming navigation of caring for a dairy- and egg- allergic child I have created this recipe compilation and tips book as a guidepost for all of those harried mothers facing the pantry and refrigerator, wondering what to cook for a meal or a snack without any dairy protein, egg protein, tree nut protein, or nut protein.

My son Evan was diagnosed soon after his initial reaction with a potentially fatal allergy to dairy and a severe allergy to eggs. So there we were, my robust, pink, healthy son in the allergist's office, hearing the words that sounded like a punishing sentence: avoid all forms of dairy, all forms of eggs, and all peanuts and tree nuts...for the time being...for now... maybe forever.

I had recognized signs. An immediate hive would appear on Evan's forehead after my older son would give him a kiss with lips straight from a bottle of milk. I noticed eczema on Evan's body hours after I would take one sip of my husband's coffee with creamer. I breastfed Evan exclusively until he was about 10 months old and carefully watched my diet. I knew a bit about the drill because my older son had issues with dairy.

He outgrew them; there is hope! I completely avoided dairy throughout the early months with Evan, but now this: I was told to not even take a chance by having any dairy in the house; his skin test reaction was so instant and severe.

So WHAT do I cook for dinner for a family of four, which includes a husband who grew up with melted butter on the dinner table?? WHAT is there to cook without adding cheese or cream of mushroom soup? WHAT am I going to make for a treat? WHAT am I going to quickly whip up for dinner when I don't have the time or energy?? WHAT am I going to serve at Evan's first birthday party??

I felt so alone: there I was, mother supreme, in charge of all the meals and treats and nutrition and food fun and suddenly I have to wipe my 'culinary experience' slate clean and start anew. I'd like to say it was easy. But having to give up the convenience foods and step away from the dairy obsessed culture has been really hard. But I must tell you: it feels perfectly normal now. No, I can't order take-out or throw together a quick omelet, but I've learned a few tricks of my own. My cooking repertoire has greatly expanded and includes many different cultural flairs. Some say my kids eat more "exotic" than their kids do. I take that to mean that my young boys enjoy foods that rely on spice for flavor instead of cheese or creams. I think overall that is beneficial to their lives--health and taste wise. The bottom line is that my boys aren't extraordinarily adventuresome and yet they think their lives are full of good food. They are not used to order-in pizza and take out meals, so they don't expect that, nor crave and demand that route. We eat a majority of unprocessed foods, which is a good thing. We rely heavily on meals with meat in them to meet their nutritional needs and to satisfy their appetites. I am constantly trying new adaptations of recipes, which appeal to kids and have discovered many great dishes to add to our meal rotation.

Two years after the diagnosis of dairy and egg allergies, Evan had a reaction to tree nuts. Tests showed a "mid-range" sensitivity to tree nuts and peanuts. I am grateful that my doctor cautioned me against any nut proteins at the initial allergy diagnosis. Sometimes kids with food allergies tend to be the "chosen" ones to have an anaphylactic reaction to nuts. And sometimes allergies to nuts show up a little later in life.

Therefore, my pantry had to be free of all dairy, egg, and nut proteins.

I have put together my collection of tried and true dairy-free, egg-free, and nut-free, kid tested and kid pleasing recipes for you with a sense of hope and camaraderie. These are the recipes that work for kids--not the recipes more geared for adult taste buds. The majority of the recipes compiled here are main dish recipes or dinner ideas, plus our very favorite goodies and baked necessities. I only included (REALLY!) the items that passed muster with my hungry preschooler and toddler. I hope it helps to relieve the stress of searching for dishes and treats that not only taste good but meet your texture expectations as well. Meals should be savored and served with love. With an allergy-appropriate recipe collection in your back pocket, you'll be back to cooking without any extra frustration.

I have also included my grand list of TIPS that includes the main points of wisdom from the working trenches of a mother living and cooking for a child with food allergies. It is my hope that you take away some new ideas, relieve some stress, and feel a sense of camaraderie. Good luck! And good cooking!

DINNERS WITH CHICKEN

Chicken Curry

This dish is one of our all time favorites! My family gobbles up this one-skillet, sweet tasting dinner.

1 Tbl. Vegetable oil
1-1½ lbs. boneless, skinless chicken breasts, cut into bite-sized pieces
3 apples, cored, peeled, and diced
1 onion, diced
5 cloves of garlic, minced
2 Tbl. curry powder, or more to taste
1½ tsp. Cumin
½ C raisins
5 C dairy-free chicken broth
salt and pepper to taste
2 C rice (not instant)

Brown the chicken in the oil in a large skillet or Dutch oven. Salt and pepper to your taste. Remove chicken with a slotted spoon and place on a plate. Set aside.

Add vegetables and curry and cumin to the pan. Sauté 8 to 10 minutes, or until tender.

Deglaze pan with a tablespoon of broth. Add remaining broth and raisins. Bring to a boil. Add rice and chicken.

Cover, reduce heat and simmer until rice is tender, about 60 minutes.

Chicken Nuggets

A kid favorite, these chicken nuggets are just as good as any fast food chain! Complete this meal with a carrot side dish and Creamy Noodles for a fun Friday night, kid-pleasing meal. My boys especially adore their "job" of crushing the crackers.

5 Tbl. dairy-free margarine
3 tsp. Worcestershire sauce
1½ to 2 lb. boneless, skinless chicken breasts, cut into 1-inch pieces
50 dairy-free, nut-free, Ritz-type crackers, finely crushed

Preheat oven to 450 degrees.

In a large, glass bowl melt the margarine and Worcestershire sauce together and then stir.

Add the chicken and toss to coat well.

Crush the crackers in a gallon-sized Ziploc plastic bag. Add the covered chicken pieces and shake to coat all pieces well. Place chicken pieces in a single layer in a 15x10x1-inch baking pan.

Bake for 8 to 10 minutes, or until no longer pink in the middle.

Serve with some dairy-free, nut-free barbeque sauce for dipping.

BBQ Chicken Pie

This dish is one of our all-time favorite meals. The 'pie' is tangy and sweet and so delicious! This pleasing meal is good enough for company--but you may not want to share. It tastes better the next day, so you'll want leftovers.

Filling
1 tsp. dairy-free margarine
2 C onions, diced
½ C green pepper, chopped
1 clove garlic, minced
1½ tsp. cumin
1 tsp. coriander
¼ C cider vinegar
1 (4.5-oz.) can diced green chilies, drained
1½ lb. cooked, shredded chicken breast (approx. 4 breast halves)
2 Tbl. brown sugar
1 oz. unsweetened baking chocolate, grated
1 (12-oz.) bottle chili sauce
11 oz. dairy-free chicken broth

Topping
1½ C flour
½ C sugar
½ C corn meal
1 Tbl. baking powder
½ tsp. salt
1¼ C plain soymilk
1½ Tbl. water, 1½ Tbl. oil, 1 tsp. baking powder; mixed together
1/3 C oil

For filling:
Preheat oven to 350 degrees. Grease a 9-inch x 13-inch baking pan.

In a large skillet or Dutch oven, sauté onion, green pepper, and garlic in the margarine for five minutes. Add cumin, coriander, and sauté for two more minutes.
Stir in vinegar, loosening any brown bits from pan, and add the rest of the filling ingredients. Cook 15 minutes, or until thick, stirring occasionally.

For topping:
Prepare when filling is thickening on the stove.

Whisk together flour, sugar, cornmeal, baking powder, and salt. Set aside in a large bowl.

Combine soymilk, water/oil/baking powder mixture, and oil.

Add wet ingredients to dry ingredients. Stir just until blended.

Spoon filling into prepared pan. Cover evenly with topping.

Bake 30 to 35 minutes, or until golden brown.

Let sit 15 minutes before serving.

Slow Cook Chicken Drumsticks

My kids are fanatic chicken leg lovers. This satisfies the savage beasts. Serve with Aunt Jean's Rice and a favorite vegetable and you'll feel good about the number of calories they devoured.

1½ to 2 lb. chicken drumsticks, rinsed well
2 Tbl. vegetable oil
2 bottles (18 oz.) dairy-free, nut-free barbeque sauce

Brown the chicken in the oil, making sure all sides get browned.

Cover the bottom of the slow cooker with barbeque sauce, add the chicken legs, and pour the rest of the sauce over the top.

Cover and cook on low for 8 to 9 hours, or on high for 4 to 5 hours, or until chicken is no longer pink on the inside.

Mandarin Chicken

This super easy meal is perfect for the busy, chaotic world with kids. It takes just minutes to prepare. Pop it in the oven and it's ready an hour later.

1½ C rice
1 lb. boneless, skinless chicken breasts
2 C orange juice
1 C dairy-free chicken broth
½ tsp. salt
pepper to taste
1 (8.5-oz.) can mandarin oranges
Paprika and minced fresh parsley, optional

Preheat oven to 375 degrees. Grease a shallow 3 qt. baking dish.

Spread uncooked rice in prepared pan. Top with chicken. Pour orange juice and broth over all. Sprinkle with salt and pepper. Top with oranges.

Bake for 65 minutes, or until chicken juices run clear and rice is tender.

Garnish with paprika and parsley, if desired.

Chicken Casablanca

This classy dinner actually passes muster with the kids!

2 Tbl. olive oil
½ small onion, diced
1 large clove of garlic, minced
¼ C red pepper, diced
¼ C green pepper, diced
1 carrot, diced
1 lb. boneless, skinless chicken breasts, cut into bite-size pieces
14 oz. dairy-free chicken broth
1 tsp. honey
salt and pepper to taste
¼ C diced pitted prunes (about 3)
1 box (5 3/4 oz.) plain nut-free, dairy-free couscous
fresh parsley or chives for garnish, chopped (optional)

In a large skillet, heat 1 tablespoon of olive oil over medium heat. Add onion and garlic; cook 30 seconds to soften. Add the peppers and the carrot; cook for about 5 minutes, stirring frequently. Remove mixture with a slotted spoon and set aside.

Brown the chicken in the remaining tablespoon of oil. Add the reserved vegetables, chicken broth, honey, salt, and pepper; bring to a boil. Reduce heat to low, add the prunes and simmer for 5 minutes, or until sauce is thick enough to coat a spoon.

Cook the couscous according to package directions.

Serve the filling over the couscous and garnish with the parsley or chives if desired.

Chicken Cacciatore

My kids gobble up anything that looks like spaghetti. This dish tastes a bit fancier than the usual marinara sauce.

2 Tbl. olive oil
1 lb. boneless, skinless chicken breasts, cut into bite-sized pieces
1 C onions, diced
½ C green peppers, chopped
½ C celery, chopped
2 cloves garlic, minced
3 to 4 C tomato sauce
1½ tsp. dried oregano
1 tsp. basil

In a large saucepan, sauté chicken and vegetables in the olive oil until chicken is no longer pink in the middle. Add tomato sauce and spices. Simmer until heated through.

Serve over your favorite pasta, spaghetti squash (surprisingly passable with my kids), or rice vermicelli.

Chicken Enchiladas

I came up with this creamy, satisfying recipe one day while yearning for the good old cheese-encrusted variety of enchiladas. I was never satisfied with the vegan cheeses, so I wanted something fulfilling without relying on the cheese factor. This dish "feels" creamy, is so satisfying, and so good.

2 Tbl. olive oil
1 lb. boneless, skinless chicken breasts, cut into bite-sized pieces
1 tsp. cumin
1 tsp. coriander
½ tsp. garlic powder
salt and pepper to taste
1 (15-oz.) can black bean refried beans
dairy free, egg free flour or corn tortillas, or a mixture of both
1 batch Mexican Sauce (following)

Heat oil in large skillet. Add chicken and season with spices. Sauté in the oil until no longer pink in the center.

Prepare Mexican Sauce (recipe following).

In a large bowl, empty the refried beans. Add cooked chicken and any secret veggies that you are including (zucchini works well diced). Add 1 C Mexican Sauce. Mix well.

Preheat oven to 350 degrees. Grease a 9-inch x 13-inch dish.

Fill tortillas with about 3 Tbl. of the mixture, roll up, and lay side by side in pan. When finished, cover with the rest of the Mexican Sauce and cook in oven for about 20 minutes, until heated through.

Mexican Sauce
2 tsp. olive oil
1 C onion, minced
½ tsp. salt
1½ tsp. cumin
2 tsp. chili powder
2 (15-oz.) cans of diced tomatoes with juice
black pepper and/or cayenne pepper, to taste
4 to 6 medium cloves of garlic, minced

Chicken Enchiladas, continued:

Heat olive oil in a medium-sized saucepan. Add onion and salt and sauté over medium heat for about 5 minutes. Add cumin and chili powder, and sauté about 5 minutes more.

Add tomatoes, pepper(s), and garlic. Bring to a boil, partially cover, and then lower heat. Simmer at least 15 minutes.

Roast Chicken

This down-home comfort food is requested and devoured at my house! Serve with Aunt Jean's Rice and some fresh vegetables and feel like Mrs. Cleaver.

1 3 ½- to 4- lb. chicken, broiler-fryer, whole
2 to 3 sprigs fresh rosemary
1 large lemon, cut into chunks, peel left on
a few pats of dairy-free margarine

Preheat oven to 375 degrees.

Thoroughly rinse chicken on the outside and the inside. Place breast-side up on a rack in a shallow roasting pan. Fill the inside cavity with rosemary and lemon chunks. Smear the top of the chicken with the margarine pats.

Bake for 1¼ to 1¾ hours, or until chicken is no longer pink on the inside. Occasionally baste the chicken with pan juices.

There are usually many different herb chicken recipes in cookbooks--try them until you hit the one that works for your family.

Easy Crock-Pot Chicken

This chicken is so easy and so delicious! A quick, simple solution for our busy lives: prepare the chicken in the morning, and then just hassle with the side dishes later that evening.

2 carrots, sliced
2 onions, thinly sliced
2 stalks celery, thinly sliced
1 (3 to 4 lb.) broiler-fryer whole chicken, rinsed well
1 tsp. salt
½ tsp. black pepper
¾ C dairy-free, egg-free chicken broth
½ tsp. basil
½ tsp. garlic powder

Place sliced vegetables on the bottom of the stoneware. Add the (rinsed) whole chicken. Top with salt and pepper. Pour broth over the top.

Sprinkle the basil and garlic powder.

Cover and cook on High for 4 to 5 hours, or on Low for 8 to 10 hours.

Stir Fry Chicken with
Sweet and Sour Sauce

This quick and easy dish is an excellent way to get your youngsters to eat vegetables.

1 lb. boneless, skinless chicken breasts, cut into bite-sized pieces
2 to 3 C sliced vegetables that your kids love
2 to 3 Tbl. olive oil
dash of sesame oil (to taste)
1 to 2 Tbl. garlic powder, to taste
1 tsp. onion powder
2 C cooked rice
Sweet and Sour Sauce (to follow)

Season the chicken with the garlic and onion powders and brown in the oils. Add vegetables right before the chicken is thoroughly browned. Sauté over medium-high heat until vegetables are tender and the chicken is no longer pink in the middle.

Serve over hot rice with sweet and sour sauce.

Sweet and Sour Sauce:
½ C packed brown sugar
1 Tbl. cornstarch
1/3 C red wine vinegar
1/3 C unsweetened pineapple juice (I stock my pantry with a small sized, six-pack of cans; kids love to "finish" the can).
1 Tbl. soy sauce
¼ tsp. garlic powder
¼ tsp. ground ginger

In a 2-cup glass-measuring cup, combine all ingredients. Cook in the microwave, uncovered, on 100% power (high) for 3 to 5 minutes or till thickened and bubbly, stirring every minute till mixture starts to thicken, then every 30 seconds. Cook 30 seconds more.

Chicken Lemon Sauté

A delicious dish with a tangy lemon teriyaki sauce.

3 boneless, skinless chicken breasts
3 Tbl. flour
¼ C dairy-free margarine
1/3 C dairy-free, nut-free Teriyaki sauce (bottled, or make your own)
3 Tbl. lemon juice (fresh is best!)
1 tsp. minced garlic
1/2 tsp. sugar
hot cooked rice

Coat chicken with flour. Melt margarine in large skillet over medium heat; add chicken. Cook until chicken is lightly browned, about 5 to 7 minutes. Turn chicken over; cook until lightly browned on the other side, about 5 to 7 minutes. Remove chicken; set aside.

Add teriyaki sauce, lemon juice, garlic, and sugar to skillet, stirring to combine. Return chicken to pan; simmer 3 minutes. Turn chicken over and cook 2 to 3 minutes, or until chicken is no longer pink in center. Serve over rice.

Chicken and Rice Casserole

This creamy and satisfying casserole has a great flavor and texture. A super way to use any leftovers from a roast chicken!

½ C dairy-free margarine
½ C flour
1 tsp. salt and pepper to taste
¼ tsp. turmeric
¼ C plain soymilk
2 C dairy-free chicken broth
1 (4 oz. can) sliced mushrooms
2 Tbl. onion, diced
3 C COOKED rice
2 C diced COOKED chicken or turkey

Preheat oven to 375 degrees.

In a medium saucepan melt margarine. Add flour, salt, pepper, and turmeric and combine well. Slowly add soymilk and chicken broth. Cook and stir until thick and smooth. Set aside.

In a large bowl, combine mushrooms, onions, cooked rice and cooked chicken. Stir in sauce until well combined. Place in a 9-inch x 13-inch pan.

Bake for about 25 minutes, until heated through and bubbly.

Chicken Shish Kebabs

We love grilling kebabs. This dish is so easy and delicious that it is often on our dinner table.

1 lb. boneless, skinless chicken breasts, cut into bite-sized pieces
marinade (see following)

Tex-Mex Marinade
6 tsp. limejuice
3 tsp. minced garlic
3 tsp. garlic powder
3 tsp. vegetable oil

Asian Marinade
6 tsp. soy sauce
3 tsp. minced garlic
3 tsp. vegetable oil
3 tsp. sesame oil

Combine the ingredients for your choice of marinade in a large, Ziploc bag.   Cut chicken into ¾ -inch cubes. Add chicken to the bag, and seal. Turn the bag until the meat is coated evenly, and then place in the refrigerator for five to ten minutes. Preheat the grill while the meat is marinating.

Remove the chicken from the bag, and discard the marinade. Using four 10-inch metal skewers, thread the chicken onto the skewers.

Grill the kebabs over medium-high heat for about four minutes per side, or until the chicken is no longer pink in the center. Remove the kebabs from the skewers and serve.

Mu Shu Chicken Wraps

This fantastically yummy and fantastically easy dish is a
favorite "Friday Night" meal. I often pack along my crock-pot
and these ingredients on a trip for a fast, easy, delicious
vacation meal.

1 medium onion, diced
1½ to 2 lb. boneless, skinless chicken thighs
salt and pepper to taste
1 (8 oz.) jar Hoisin sauce (Asian section of the supermarket/I
use Sun Luck brand)
2 Tbl. honey
¼ tsp. ground ginger
1 (12 oz.) bag broccoli coleslaw mix, or chopped cabbage
dairy-free flour tortillas

Place the diced onions in the crock-pot. Season the rinsed
chicken thighs with salt and pepper and then place on top of
the onions.

Cook on low for 7 to 8 hours, or until the meat easily shreds.
Remove chicken and onions with a slotted spoon and place in
a large bowl. Shred the meat with two forks in the bowl.

Combine the Hoisin sauce, honey and ginger in a small bowl.
Add to the chicken mixture and mix well.

Place a couple spoonfuls of the chicken mixture on a warm
tortilla; add a handful of broccoli coleslaw and roll up for your
taste bud delight.

Teriyaki Chicken Kebabs

This delicious thick glaze clings to the chicken when you grill it, giving the meat a great flavor. You can use it for shrimp, beef, pork, or scallops as well. Serve it with a cold Yakisoba noodle salad (see below) and a vegetable for a great meal.

Teriyaki glaze:
¼ C soy sauce
3 Tbl. brown sugar
1½ Tbl. rice vinegar
1 tsp. ground ginger
¼ tsp. crushed red pepper
1 clove garlic, minced
1½ tsp. cornstarch
1½ tsp. water
meat: chicken, shrimp, beef, pork, or scallops

Whisk together the cornstarch and water until smooth. Combine all ingredients in a small saucepan. Bring to a boil over medium-high heat. Cook for about 2 minutes, until thickened. Cool.

Cut meat into bite-sized chunks and thread onto skewers. Brush with some olive oil and place on grill that has been coated with cooking spray. Cook for about 3 minutes. Turn the kebabs and brush with half of the teriyaki glaze. Turn once more and brush with remaining glaze. Cook until meat is no longer pink in the middle.

Yakisoba noodles: rinse a packaged bag of noodles in warm water to separate. Toss with some orange juice, sesame oil, a touch of soy sauce, and chopped green onions. Chill in the refrigerator until served.

Tarragon Chicken Bun Boats

These fun little buns are sure to be a hit with your whole family. The tarragon lends a subtle, savory flavor.

2 Tbl. flour
1 C plain soymilk
1 C dairy-free chicken broth
1 Tbl. olive oil
2/3 C sweet onion, minced
1 lb. skinless, boneless chicken breast, cut into bite-sized pieces
1 C carrots, diced
1 C zucchini, diced
½ tsp. salt
½ tsp. dried tarragon
½ tsp. black pepper
large homemade biscuits (see biscuit recipe)

In a medium sized bowl, whisk flour, soymilk, and chicken broth together until well blended. Set aside.

In a large skillet, sauté chicken and onion in the oil over medium-high heat for about 4 minutes. Add carrots, zucchini, and spices. Cover, reduce heat and cook for about 4 more minutes.

Stir in broth mixture. Bring to a boil; cover, reduce heat, and simmer until thick (about 10 minutes), stirring occasionally.

Prepare biscuit dough as directed in the bread section. To create "boats," form about 3 tablespoons of dough into a rectangle shape. The recipe should create 5 boats. Bake as directed.

Scoop out the middle section of the biscuits, creating "boats." Fill each "boat" with about 1 C chicken mixture. Serve to smiles!

Chicken Mole

This quick and easy dinner is perfect for a hectic night.

1 tsp. olive oil
1 medium onion, diced
2 cloves garlic, minced
¾ C dairy-free chicken broth
1 (8 oz.) can tomato sauce
1 ripe banana, mashed
1 Tbl. chili powder
1 Tbl. unsweetened cocoa powder
1 tsp. ground cinnamon
1 tsp. cumin
¼ tsp. black pepper
¼ tsp. cayenne powder
4 boneless, skinless chicken breast halves, cut into 1-inch pieces
hot cooked rice
warm, dairy-free, flour or corn tortillas

Sauté onion and garlic in the olive oil in a large skillet over medium-high heat until onion is browned. Deglaze pan with 1 Tbl. of the chicken broth.

Add tomato sauce, remaining broth, banana, and spices. Bring to a boil; reduce heat and simmer, covered, for 10 minutes.

Add chicken. Continue to simmer until chicken is no longer pink in the middle, about 15 minutes longer.

Serve burrito style, with a scoop of hot rice, in tortillas, with some soy-sour-cream for dipping.

Chicken Pot Pie

This easy, delicious dish tastes just like the yummy frozen chicken pot pies our mothers would get us on Friday nights for a treat. Healthy and satisfying, this pie has earned its proud place in our weekly meal rotation.

Filling:
3 C dairy-free, egg-free chicken broth
2 tsp. dried parsley
¾ C onion, minced
½ C celery, minced
2 C thinly sliced carrots
1 C green beans
1 C peas
1/3 C flour
½ C water
2 to 3 C COOKED chicken breasts, chopped into bite-sized pieces
salt and pepper to taste

Topping:
2 C flour
½ tsp. salt
½ tsp. dried thyme
2 tsp. baking powder
½ C cold dairy-free margarine
1 C plain soymilk

In a large saucepan over medium-high heat, combine broth, parsley, and onion, celery, carrots, and green beans. Bring to a boil and then simmer until vegetables are tender. Add peas.

Preheat oven to 400 degrees.

Whisk together flour and water until smooth; stir into the vegetable mixture until it becomes thickened. Add chicken pieces and remove from heat.

Add desired amount of salt and pepper. Pour the mixture into a 9-inch x 13-inch baking dish. Bake for 20 minutes.

While the chicken mixture is baking, whisk flour, salt, thyme, and baking powder together in a large bowl. Cut in margarine with a pastry blender until it resembles crumbs. Stir in soymilk until dough forms.

Drop topping by tablespoonfuls on top of partially cooked chicken mixture. Spread out each dough blob with two spoons, so dough is spread out to a uniform thickness, covering the filling.

Return chicken pot pie to the oven and bake for an additional 20 minutes, until topping is golden brown.

Chicken Paprikash Potatoes

Richly satisfying, this easy dinner is a family winner.

Baking potatoes—enough for your family
1 lb. boneless, skinless chicken breasts, cut into bite-sized pieces
2 Tbl. flour
2 tsp. paprika
¾ tsp. salt
1/8 tsp. red pepper flakes
2 Tbl. dairy-free margarine
½ C onion, minced
2 garlic cloves, minced
½ C dairy-free, egg-free chicken broth
¼ C soy sour cream substitute

Bake potatoes in 350 degree oven until soft. Keep warm until use.

Place flour, paprika, salt and pepper flakes in a large Ziploc bag, add chicken pieces and shake until well coated.

Melt margarine in a large skillet or Dutch oven. Add chicken mixture, onion, and garlic and sauté about 5 minutes. Add broth and bring to a boil. Cook until chicken is done and the sauce is thickened, about 6 minutes. Remove from heat and stir in soy-sour cream substitute.

Top the potato with chicken mixture. Sprinkle with fresh or dried parsley if desired.

Crock Pot Chicken Cassoulet

Here is another easy, hearty crock pot dish.

1 C dry navy beans: prepared (directions below)
2 pounds chicken pieces: breast, thigh, or drumsticks
1 pound cooked Polish sausage ring
1 C tomato juice
1 Tbl. Worcestershire sauce
1 tsp. beef or chicken bouillon
½ tsp. basil
½ tsp. oregano
½ tsp. paprika
½ C carrot, diced
½ C celery, diced
½ C onion, diced

Rinse dry beans well and place in a large saucepan. Fill pan with water. Bring to a boil; reduce heat and simmer for 10 minutes. Remove beans from heat and let stand, covered, for 1 hour. Or soak beans in water overnight. Drain.

Rinse and cut chicken into desired sized pieces. Cut sausage into 1-inch pieces.

In a medium bowl, combine prepared beans, tomato juice, Worcestershire sauce, bouillon, basil, oregano, and paprika.

In the crock pot place the diced carrot, celery, and onion. Place the chicken and sausage over the vegetables. Pour the flavored bean mixture over the meat.

Cover and cook on low setting for 9 to 11 hours or for 5 to 5½ hours on the high setting.

Remove meat with a slotted spoon. Lightly mash remaining mixture. Serve meat in bowls with bean mixture spooned over the top. Can serve with soy sour cream substitute.

Chicken Strips

Here is a dairy-free, egg-free version of this kid-pleasing dish!
Serve with "safe" barbeque sauce and delight your child.

1 lb. chicken breast, cut into ½-inch diagonal strips
1 C plain soymilk
3 Tbl. dairy-free margarine
¼ tsp. salt
2 to 3 C dairy-free, egg-free, nut-free corn flake type cereal

Preheat oven to 400 degrees. Lightly grease a baking sheet.

Heat the soymilk and margarine in a small saucepan until
margarine is melted. Add salt and mix well.   Pour into a
shallow dish.

Crush the cereal in a large Ziploc bag with a rolling pin. Pour
cereal crumbs into a shallow dish.

Dip the chicken slices into the soymilk mixture and then the
cereal mixture. Coat the chicken slices well. Place in a single
layer onto prepared baking sheet.

Lightly coat the chicken slices with cooking spray.

Bake, uncovered, for 15 to 18 minutes, until chicken is no
longer pink in the middle.

If you have leftovers, reheat in the oven to re-crisp the cereal.
These get soggy reheated in the microwave!

DINNERS WITH BEEF

Beef Curry

This sweet and delicious dish is a bit different than the chicken curry.

1½ lbs. chuck steak
½ C flour
1 tsp. salt
2 medium onions, diced
3 large apples, diced
1 tomato, chopped
1 clove garlic, minced
¼ C dairy-free margarine
2 Tbl. curry powder
2 C dairy-free beef broth
2 Tbl. lemon juice (fresh is best)
½ C raisins
1 tsp. sugar
3 Tbl. flaked, sweetened, coconut
hot cooked rice

Cut the meat into small pieces; roll it in the flour seasoned with salt. Peel and chop onions, apples, and tomato into small pieces; set aside.

In a large skillet, brown the meat in the margarine. When brown, add onions, apples, tomato, and garlic. Cook for 8 to 10 minutes more, until tender. Pour off any excess fat.

Add the curry powder and any flour left after coating the meat. Mix well and stir in the broth.

Add lemon juice, raisins, sugar, and coconut. Simmer for one hour.

Serve over hot rice.

Slow Cooker Beef Goulash

This is Evan's favorite meal and I must say it ranks high in my "comfort" food list. Set this up in the morning alongside your Bread machine and be the hero at dinner!

1 lb. ground beef (or ground turkey)
2 cans (10 3/4 oz. each) condensed tomato soup, undiluted
2 C uncooked macaroni
1 can (16 oz.) corn, drained
½ C onion, diced
1 can (4 oz.) sliced mushrooms, drained
2 Tbl. ketchup
1 Tbl. mustard
Salt and pepper to taste
any "secret" vegetables: zucchini works well

Brown beef in skillet, drain fat. Transfer to slow cooker.

Add remaining ingredients to slow cooker. Stir to blend.

Cover and cook on Low 7 to 9 hours or on High for 3 to 4 hours.

Empanadas

This dish is now a family favorite. The meaty, calzone-type entree tastes exotic, sweet, and tangy. It reheats well (and tastes great piping hot wrapped in foil on a sledding trip the day after!).

1/3 C raisins
1 Tbl. apple cider vinegar
1 lb. lean ground beef
1 small onion, diced
2 cloves garlic, minced
16 oz. salsa, divided
2 Tbl. packed brown sugar
½ tsp. ground cinnamon
¼ tsp. salt
2 (1 lb. each) loaves bread dough (I use my bread machine in the morning.)
olive oil for brushing

Combine raisins and vinegar in small bowl; soak for 15 to 20 minutes or until raisins are plump.

Preheat oven to 350 degrees. Grease baking sheet.

Cook beef, onion, and garlic in large skillet until beef is brown. Add prepared raisins, ½ C salsa, brown sugar, cinnamon, and salt. Cook, stirring frequently, for 5 to 10 minutes, or until flavors are blended.

Divide each bread dough loaf into 6 pieces; shape into balls. On well-floured board, roll each ball into a 6-inch circle. Place ¼ C beef filling on bottom half of each circle. Fold top half of dough over filling; crimp edges with tines of fork. Pierce tops with fork. Place on prepared baking sheet; brush with olive oil.

Bake for 20 to 25 minutes or until golden brown. Serve with remaining salsa.

Beef and Broccoli

Oh ye that miss Chinese Take Out Food--take heed and prepare this dish for your delectable delight. This dish tastes like the real thing--but no chance of dairy or egg noodles!

2 Tbl. plus 2 tsp. sesame oil
Juice of ½ lemon
1 Tbl. soy sauce, mixed with 1 Tbl. water
1 clove garlic, minced
1 tsp. ground ginger
1¼ lb. beef sirloin, cut across the grain: ¾- x ¼- inch strips
1 head broccoli, chopped small
2 tsp. cornstarch
1 ½ C dairy-free beef broth
1 Tbl. apple juice concentrate, thawed
hot cooked rice

Whisk 2 Tbl. sesame oil, lemon juice, and soy sauce mix together. Add garlic, ginger, and beef strips; marinate at room temperature for about 30 minutes.

Meanwhile, steam broccoli, then drain and set aside.

Dissolve cornstarch in a little beef broth, add remaining broth and apple juice and stir well.

Drain beef; discard the marinade. Brown the beef in 2 tsp. sesame oil in a large skillet or Dutch oven. Remove meat with a slotted spoon and set aside.

Add beef broth mixture to the pan, bring to a boil, and stir until thickened. Add beef and broccoli and heat through.

Serve over hot rice.

Slow Cooked Chili

This dairy- and egg- free chili is a hearty, delicious meal, perfect for a cold day. Make some sweet cornbread for the side and they'll leave the table with full bellies.

1 lb. ground beef
1 C onion, diced
½ C green pepper, diced
2 cans (15 oz.) kidney beans, rinsed and drained
1 can (14.5 oz.) diced tomatoes, drained
1 can (15 oz.) tomato sauce
2 to 3 Tbl. chili powder (to taste)
1 to 2 Tbl. sugar (to taste)

Brown beef, onion, and green pepper in skillet until beef is no longer pink and vegetables are tender; drain.

Add mixture to slow cooker. Add remaining ingredients. Stir well.

Cook on Low for 6 to 7 hours or on High for 3 to 4 hours.

Also works well in large skillet or Dutch oven on the stovetop, stirring often at a simmer for about 15 minutes to an hour.

Pot Roast

My young kids relish this traditional meal. Sunday afternoons or anytime--this meal satisfies the whole soul. This is the old fashioned method that tastes DIVINE! The extra work makes for extra taste.

5 large potatoes, peeled and chopped into 1½ -inch pieces
5 Tbl. olive oil (divided)
3 tsp. salt (divided)
¾ tsp. ground pepper (divided)
1 Tbl. dried parsley
1 Tbl. dried thyme
1 bay leaf
1 Tbl. flour
½ tsp. paprika
½ tsp. allspice
1 (3 to 3½ -pound) beef rump roast
1 large onion, chopped into large pieces
3 cloves garlic, minced
6 C dairy-free beef broth
2 Tbl. tomato paste
6 large carrots, chopped into 1-inch pieces

Preheat oven to 400 degrees.

Place potatoes in a large roasting pan, and toss with 3 Tbl. olive oil. Season potatoes with 2 tsp. salt and ¼ tsp. pepper. Roast until golden brown and crisp, 30 to 40 minutes. Remove pan from oven; set aside. Reduce oven temperature to 350 degrees.

Gather parsley, thyme, and bay leaf into a square of cheesecloth, close with string, and then set aside.

Combine flour, remaining 1 tsp. salt and remaining ½ tsp. pepper, paprika, and allspice in a small bowl. Rinse the roast and pat dry. Sprinkle seasoned flour mixture over meat, and pat to coat well.

Brown the roast in a Dutch oven or large skillet, on all sides until golden brown, over medium heat. Transfer to a plate; set aside.

Reduce heat to medium-low. Add onions and garlic, and cook, stirring occasionally, until onions are tender. Transfer roast, onions, garlic, pan drippings, cheesecloth spice bundle, beef stock, and tomato paste to a large roasting pan (or combine all in the Dutch oven).

Cover, and place in oven for 30 minutes. Turn the roast over, and cook for 30 more minutes.

Add carrots, cover, and return to oven for 1½ hours, turning the roast over every 30 minutes.

Add roasted potatoes to pan, submerging them halfway in the stock mixture. Return roast to oven, leaving pan uncovered, for 30 minutes more.

Notes: *Total roasting time for roast is 3 hours.
*Don't forget the roasting time for the potatoes is an earlier, 40 minutes.

Chili Mac

Easy and kid pleasing, Chili Mac hits the spot. Serve with a side of Corn Bread.

1 lb. ground beef
½ onion, diced
2 C uncooked macaroni
1 (15-oz.) can kidney beans, drained and well rinsed
1 (15-oz.) can tomato sauce
1 tsp. chili powder (or to taste)
1 tsp. salt

Brown beef and onion in a large skillet until beef is no longer pink. Drain. Add macaroni, kidney beans, tomato sauce, chili powder, and salt.

Cover and simmer 15 to 20 minutes, or until noodles are tender. You might need to add a bit of water.

Spaghetti

I have always preferred to make my own red sauce. With Evan's allergies, I completely gave up the bottled sauces. This is my tried and true (and quick!) sauce that my kids crave. I always serve my drop biscuits with this dinner.

1 lb. ground beef
¾ C onion, diced
5 cloves garlic, minced
¾ C zucchini, diced
½ C green or red pepper, diced
1 can (14.5 oz.) diced tomatoes (with juice)
1 can (15 oz.) tomato sauce
1 bay leaf
1 Tbl. oregano
1 Tbl. basil
1 Tbl. sugar

Brown beef, onion, garlic, zucchini, and red/green peppers in large skillet or saucepan, drain. Add can of diced tomatoes with juice, tomato sauce, bay leaf, oregano, basil, and sugar. Bring to a boil.

Reduce heat; cover, and simmer for at least 20 to 30 minutes. A longer simmer times boosts a more intense flavor.

Serve over fun, hot noodles, with biscuits on the side.

Jambalaya

This is another one of our favorite meals and it has become a potluck favorite among our extended family. A fresh loaf of bread is a perfect accompaniment. There is a hint of spiciness, but the boys really go for it.

2 Tbl. dairy-free margarine
1 medium onion, diced
1 C green or red pepper, diced
2 cloves garlic, minced
1 (1 lb.) dairy-free, Kielbasa sausage, cut into ¼ -inch slices
1 C uncooked rice
2 C dairy-free chicken broth
2 Tbl. green pepper sauce (bottled, found by the hot sauces at the store), adjust to your family's taste
1 (14.5-oz.) can diced tomatoes, drained

Melt margarine in a large skillet or Dutch oven over medium-high heat. Add onion, green/red pepper, garlic, and sausage slices and cook for 10-12 minutes, or until vegetables are tender, stirring often.

Stir in rice, chicken broth, green pepper sauce, and tomatoes; mix well and bring to a boil.

Reduce heat, cover, and simmer 25 minutes, or until rice is tender, stirring occasionally.

Swedish Meatballs

A creamy, satisfying dish that does not feel deprived without the dairy and eggs.

2¼ C plain soymilk (divided)
¾ C soft homemade bread crumbs (1 slice) OR use "safe"
Corn Flakes or Crispy Rice cereal crumbs
½ C onion, diced
1/8 C dried parsley flakes
3/8 tsp. black pepper (divided)
1/8 tsp. allspice
1 lb. ground beef
3 Tbl. dairy-free margarine
2 Tbl. flour
2 tsp. instant dairy-free beef bouillon granules
hot cooked dairy-free, egg-free noodles

In bowl combine ¼ C soymilk, the breadcrumbs or cereal crumbs, onion, parsley, ¼ tsp. pepper, and the allspice. Add meat; mix well. Shape into 30 meatballs.

In a large skillet over medium heat, cook meatballs in margarine half at a time until the balls are no longer pink on the inside. Turn to brown evenly. Drain meatballs on paper towels. Reserve 2 Tbl. drippings in skillet.

Stir flour, bouillon granules, and 1/8 tsp. pepper into the reserved drippings. Add remaining soymilk. Cook and stir until thickened and bubbly. Cook and stir 1 minute more. Return meatballs to skillet. Heat through.

Serve over hot "safe" noodles.

Meatloaf

Finally--a kid pleasing, egg-free meatloaf that has a great texture AND taste! My husband even loves this loaf--and he wasn't fond of meatloaf before tasting this. I like to serve mashed sweet potatoes with this dish.

¼ C onions, diced
2 cloves garlic, minced
1 C cooked, pureed vegetables (mushrooms, carrots, broccoli, celery, zucchini, green or red peppers, any vegetable would work-use your left-overs)
1 lb. ground beef
1 C homemade breadcrumbs

Preheat oven to 375 degrees.

Sauté onions and garlic in a little olive oil. Steam or boil your choice of vegetables--just eyeball the amount, you want to end up with 1 C of puree. Puree the sautéed onions and garlic and the cooked vegetables in a blender or food processor.

In a large glass bowl, mix together the ground beef, breadcrumbs, and pureed vegetables.

Spread the beef mixture in a glass pie plate; make a hole in the middle, to collect any grease.

Bake for 30 to 35 minutes, or until there is no pink in the middle of the beef round (this method sure beats the time required for a loaf pan!).

As always--serve with some ketchup and mashed potatoes.

Tamale Pie

My kids can't decide if they like this recipe or our regular enchiladas better. They both taste down-home, comforting good to me. The crust tastes and feels like real tamales.

Filling:
1lb. ground beef
1 C onion, diced
2 cloves garlic, minced
2 C dairy-free enchilada sauce, or 1 can (15 oz.) tomato sauce, plus 1 Tbl. dairy-free taco seasoning (or to taste)
1 C corn (frozen, canned, or fresh)
1 (2 1/4-ounce) can sliced olives
1 tsp. salt
Crust:
2¼ C corn meal
2 C water
1¼ C plain soymilk
2 Tbl. dairy-free margarine
1 tsp. arrowroot powder
1 tsp. salt
1 (4-ounce) can diced green chilies

Cook beef, onion, and garlic in a large skillet until beef is brown; drain. Stir in enchilada sauce, corn, olives, and salt.

Preheat oven to 425 degrees. Grease an 8-inch x 11-inch baking dish.

Combine corn meal, water, soymilk, margarine, arrowroot powder, and salt in a medium saucepan to prepare the crust. Cook over medium-high heat, stirring frequently, for 5 to 7 minutes, or until thickened. Stir in chilies.

Reserve 2 C corn meal mixture. Spread remaining corn meal mixture on bottom and up sides of prepared baking dish.

Bake tamale crust for 10 minutes. Remove from oven and spoon beef filling into hot crust. Spread reserved corn meal mixture over filling.

Bake for another 15 to 20 minutes.

Chili Verde

I particularly love to serve easily prepared meals that my family loves (who doesn't?). This is a great crock-pot meal. Serve with some hot tortillas on the side for rolling up and dipping.

1½ lb. boneless beef chuck, cut into 1" cubes
1½ lb. boneless lean pork loin or shoulder, cut into 1" cubes
3 Tbl. olive oil
¼ C onion, diced
1 medium green pepper, coarsely chopped
1 large clove garlic, minced
3 cans (14.5 oz. each) diced tomatoes, with juice
1 (4 oz.) can diced green chilies
¼ C parsley flakes
1 tsp. sugar
¼ tsp. ground cloves
2 tsp. cumin
¼ C lemon juice (fresh is best)
salt to taste

In a large skillet brown the beef and pork in the olive oil.

Combine the meat with the rest of the ingredients in a crock-pot and cook on low 8 to 9 hours, or on high 4 to 5 hours.

Roll up the Chili Verde in tortillas and dip in salsa or soy sour cream substitute.

Hot cooked rice on the side is nice.

Slow Cooker Beef Stew

Beef Stew was made for the crock-pot and the busy mother!
My family goes crazy for this home-cooked hot and healthy
meal. I love to serve my drop biscuits with this.

1 lb. stew beef, cut into bite-sized chunks
1 large onion, diced
2 medium carrots, peeled and thinly sliced
2 large potatoes, cut into ½-inch chunks
1 C turnip or rutabaga, diced
1 C fresh green beans, in bite-sized pieces
1 bay leaf
½ tsp. dried thyme
1 clove garlic, minced
3 C dairy-free beef broth
2 Tbl. brown sugar
¾ tsp. salt
2 tsp. Worcestershire sauce
pepper to taste
3 Tbl. all-purpose flour
2 tsp. tomato paste

Combine all of the ingredients, except the flour and tomato
paste, in a crock-pot.

Cook on low for 8 to 9 hours, or on high for 4 to 5 hours, or
until the beef and potatoes are tender.

At the last 30 minutes of cooking, combine ½ C of broth from
the crock-pot with the flour and tomato paste in a small bowl.
Whisk until smooth and then add back to the crock-pot.

Shepherd's Pie

A semester in England introduced me to this dish. It is the perfect family meal—easy preparation for mom and clean plates from the kids.

4 medium potatoes
2 to 3 Tbl. plain soymilk
2 Tbl. dairy-free margarine
1 lb. ground beef
½ C onion, diced
1 (10 oz. package) of mixed frozen vegetables
1 (10 ¾ oz.) can condensed tomato soup
1 tsp. Worcestershire sauce
¼ tsp. dried thyme
paprika

Prepare mashed potatoes. Boil peeled and quartered potatoes in water until soft. Drain potatoes and return to pan. Mash potatoes with a hand masher. Add soymilk and margarine and continue mashing until creamy.

Preheat oven to 375 degrees.

Cook beef and onion in a large skillet until meat is brown. Drain grease from pan. Run cold water over the frozen vegetables until they separate; drain. Add vegetables and ¼ C water to the skillet with the beef. Cover and cook until vegetables are tender, about 10 minutes. Stir in the soup, Worcestershire sauce, and thyme.

Transfer mixture to a casserole-baking dish. Spread mashed potatoes evenly over the top of the hot mixture. Sprinkle with paprika.

Bake for 25 to 30 minutes, until hot.

Flank Steak

This cut of beef is particularly lean and particularly delicious. The preparation that my family enjoys is easy as well.

1-1½ lb. flank steak
4 Tbl. Balsamic Vinegar
1 Tbl. garlic powder
1 Tbl. Kosher salt
½ tsp. freshly ground black peppercorn

Prepare the meat in the morning. Pour the Balsamic vinegar in a shallow baking dish. Place the meat on top of the vinegar. Sprinkle the garlic powder, Kosher salt, and pepper evenly on top of the flank steak. Cover the dish and place it in the refrigerator for the day.

Preheat oven to Broil. Move the oven rack to the top position.

Place the prepared meat in the center of a broiling pan. Discard the leftover marinade.

Broil until desired doneness; turning steak over halfway. I broil our steak for about 4 to 5 minutes and then turn it over for an additional 5 minutes. Remember that flank steak is usually a thin cut, so broiling times should be minimal.

Cut the meat up in very small pieces and serve it with ketchup, of course!

Korean Barbecued Beef Strips

This version of my husband's favorite childhood dish is a hit with our kids. The nice Asian flavor is a nice alternative for dinner.

1 (1½ to 2 lb.) beef flank steak
½ C soy sauce
2 Tbl. sesame oil
3 Tbl. sugar
1/3 C green onions, thinly sliced
3 cloves garlic, minced

Slice steak into ¾-inch strips, cutting across the grain.

Combine soy sauce, sesame oil, sugar, green onions, and garlic in a medium bowl.

Add steak strips to a shallow bowl. Pour marinade over the beef, being sure to cover meat completely. Cover. Place in the refrigerator for several hours.

Transfer meat and marinade to a Dutch oven. Cook over medium-high heat until beef strips are no longer pink in the middle. Stir occasionally.

Remove beef with a slotted spoon. Cut meat into small bite-sized pieces and serve with prepared Yakisoba noodles (Asian section of the supermarket) and oven roasted red peppers for a fabulous meal.

Hamburger Gravy

This farmer's meal of "stick to your ribs" gravy over biscuits will make your little one in overalls full and happy. This quick meal is easy and satisfying!

½- to ¾- pound ground round or ground beef
1 Tbl. dairy free margarine
2 Tbl. flour
1 dairy free beef bouillon/1 tsp. beef base (concentrated)
1/8 tsp. black pepper
1 2/3 C plain soymilk

Thoroughly brown ground beef in large saucepan. Remove beef with a slotted spoon; set aside.

Add the dairy free margarine, flour, beef bouillon, and pepper; combine.

Add plain soymilk all at once.

Stir over medium heat until thick and bubbling. Cook one additional minute.

Mix in ground beef and serve over biscuits (see recipe in Muffins & Breads) or "safe" toast.

One-Pot Beef and Rice

This simple, hearty meal is big hit with my boys.

1 Tbl. vegetable oil
1 lb. Top beef round, cut into bite-sized pieces
¾ C onion, diced
2 cloves garlic, diced
1 (4 oz.) can mushrooms
1 C carrots, thinly sliced
1 1/3 C Calrose rice
1 C orange juice
1 C beef broth
1 can Mandarin Oranges, cut into bite-sized pieces

Add oil, beef, and onion to a Dutch oven or large saucepan. Cook and stir over medium-high heat for five minutes.

Stir in garlic, mushrooms, and carrots and cook for an additional five minutes.

Add rice, orange juice, and beef broth; bring to a boil. Reduce heat, cover and simmer for twenty minutes, or until liquid has been absorbed and rice is tender.

Serve with Mandarin Orange pieces on top for a delicious meal.

DINNERS WITH PORK

Creamed Pork on Toast Points

This pork gravy over toast is a super way to use leftovers. I always make an extra couple of pork chops so I can make this dish the next day. My boys absolutely love it!

cooked pork chops (approximately ½ lb.), cut into bite-sized pieces
2 Tbl. oil
2 Tbl. flour
1 dairy-free, egg-free chicken bouillon
1/8 tsp. pepper
1 2/3 C plain soymilk
toast: made from homemade bread

In a Dutch oven or large saucepan sauté the cooked pork pieces in the oil, creating some good pan drippings. Remove meat with a slotted spoon and set aside.

Stir in the flour, bouillon, and pepper to the pan drippings. Add plain soymilk all at once. Stir over medium heat until thickened and bubbly. Cook an additional minute.

Return pork pieces to the gravy and stir to combine. Serve over toast strips.

Slow Cook Pork Ribs

This is Leighton's favorite meal of all time. I hear an ongoing chorus of "I love you mommy for making this!" every time I make it. A meat dish couldn't be easier to make either! I serve it with Aunt Jean's Rice and a yummy vegetable (corn on the cob is perfect).

2 to 2½ lbs. of boneless pork ribs
1 to 2 Tbl. vegetable oil
2 bottles (18 oz.) of dairy-free, nut-free barbeque sauce (we use Kraft Barbeque Sauce varieties)
dairy-free, egg-free, nut-free buns (optional)

Trim ribs of excess fat. Cut meat into manageable pieces.

Brown ribs on all sides, in a large skillet in the oil.

Coat the bottom of the slow cooker with barbeque sauce, add ribs, and then pour the rest of the sauce over the top.

Cook on Low for 7 to 8 hours or on High for 3 to 4 hours.

Serve on its own, or shredded in a bun.

Baked Ham

This meal is the good ole Sunday afternoon standby that my kids adore. Ham makes for a fabulous meal and tasty leftovers for sandwiches and for the freezer.

There are so many delicious spiral-cut hams that come with their own seasonings that I have become thoroughly spoiled. I scrutinize the ingredients and then purchase a nice-sized, bone-in, spiral cut ham and enjoy it for its ease and wonderful taste. The enclosed directions are always easy to follow.

Scalloped Potatoes with Ham

This recipe for dairy-free scalloped potatoes tastes and feels like the "real thing!" I add ham chunks and vegetables to make this more of a casserole meal. Prepare this without the extras for a home-cooked favorite side dish.

1/2 C onion, diced
4 Tbl. dairy-free margarine
4 Tbl. flour
1 tsp. salt
¼ tsp. pepper
2½ C plain soymilk
6 medium potatoes, peeled and thinly sliced
½ lb. (or more) fully cooked ham chunks, cut into bite-sized pieces
veggies if you wish: corn or diced zucchini work well

Preheat oven to 375 degrees. Grease a 3-quart casserole dish.

Sauté onion in margarine until tender. Stir in flour, salt and pepper. Add plain soymilk all at once. Cook and stir until thick and bubbly. Remove from heat.

Place half of the potatoes in the prepared dish. Place half of the ham and vegetables (if including) over the potatoes. Cover with half the sauce. Repeat layers.

Bake, covered, for 35 minutes.

Uncover; bake 30 more minutes or until potatoes are tender. Let stand for a few minutes before serving.

Bacon Pasties

A kid friendly, calzone-type finger food that my kids love to dip and devour.

½ lb. potatoes, diced
1 small onion, diced
1 lb. bacon, fully crisp cooked and diced
1 tsp. salt
½ tsp. pepper
pastry crust (to follow)
olive oil

Preheat oven to 425 degrees.

Mix the chopped potatoes, onion, and cooked bacon in a large bowl. Add salt and pepper; mix well.

Divide the crust into 8 balls. Roll each ball into a circle. Place an eighth of the filling on each circle and fold over. Press well and crimp edges with a fork. Prick the top with a fork. Brush with some olive oil.

Bake about 30 minutes, or until golden brown.

Pastry crust:
4 C flour
1 tsp. salt
½ C dairy-free margarine
½ C vegetable shortening
4 Tbl. cold water

Whisk flour and salt together in a large bowl. Cut in the margarine and shortening until the mixture looks like fine breadcrumbs.
Add water and mix to a firm dough. Knead lightly until bowl is clean. Use as directed above.

Possible dips: dairy-free, nut-free barbeque sauce, soy sour cream substitute, sweet and sour sauce (see chicken stir fry with sweet and sour sauce)

Honey Mustard Pork Chops

These chops are fancy enough for company and quick to prepare.

¼ C grainy mustard
1/3 C regular or Dijon mustard (to your taste)
3 Tbl. honey
½ slice homemade bread, torn into fine crumbs
1/3 C wheat bran
2 Tbl. dried parsley
¾ tsp. garlic powder, or more to taste
8 small loin pork chops (½ -inch thick, about 2½ lbs. total)
4 Tbl. olive oil, divided
¼ tsp. black pepper
3 Tbl. dairy-free margarine, melted

Preheat oven to 375 degrees.

In a shallow bowl, whisk together the mustards and honey. In another shallow bowl, combine the breadcrumbs, wheat bran, parsley, and garlic powder.

In a large skillet, warm 2 Tbl. oil over medium-high heat. Sprinkle the chops with pepper. Add 4 chops to the pan and sear for 1 to 2 minutes per side.

With tongs, dip the chops one at a time into the honey mustard mixture, coating both sides. Then place each chop in the herb-crumb mixture to coat, pressing the crumbs into the chops to make them adhere. Place the chops in a single layer in a large baking pan.

In the same skillet, warm the remaining 2 Tbl. oil and repeat with the remaining chops and coating mixtures.

Drizzle the chops with the melted margarine and bake them for about 20 minutes, or until a crust forms on top and the pork chops are no longer pink in the middle. Serve hot.

Chili Verde

I particularly love to serve easily prepared meals that my family loves (who doesn't?). This is a great crock-pot meal. Serve with some hot tortillas on the side for rolling up and dipping.

1½ lb. boneless beef chuck cut into 1" cubes
1½ lb. boneless lean pork loin or shoulder, cut into 1" cubes
3 Tbl. olive oil
¼ C onion, diced
1 medium green pepper, coarsely chopped
1 large clove garlic, minced
3 cans (14.5 oz. each) diced tomatoes, with juice
1 (4 oz.) can diced green chilies
¼ C dried parsley flakes
1 tsp. sugar
¼ tsp. ground cloves
2 tsp. cumin
¼ C lemon juice (fresh is best!)
salt to taste

Brown the meat in the olive oil.

Combine the meat with the rest of the ingredients in a crock-pot, mixing well, and cook on low 8 to 9 hours, or on high 4 to 5 hours.

Enjoy with warm tortillas, salsa, soy sour cream substitute, and refried beans on the side.

DINNERS WITH SEAFOOD

Shrimp and Pasta

Sweet shrimp are irresistible in this easy pasta dish.

4 Tbl. dairy-free margarine
2 Tbl. olive oil
½ C onion, diced
5 to 7 cloves of minced garlic (to taste)
1 lb. peeled and de-veined shrimp
egg-free angel hair pasta
dash of sea salt

Cook needed amount of pasta according to package directions. Keep warm until shrimp is finished cooking.

Melt margarine and olive oil over medium-high heat in a large skillet. Add onion and garlic; sauté until vegetables are just about tender.

Add shrimp and continue sautéing and stirring until shrimp is pink and ready to be devoured.

Toss the shrimp and all of the margarine drippings from the skillet with the pasta.

Sprinkle a dash of sea salt over the top and serve immediately.

Poached Salmon

This easy, delicious dish is a hit in my family. The salmon is quickly prepared and quickly eaten.

1 Tbl. cold dairy-free margarine
1-1½ lbs. boneless salmon fillets (8 ounces each)
2 C dairy-free chicken broth
salt and pepper
3 Tbl. dried dill

Preheat oven to 400 degrees.

Coat the bottom of a shallow baking dish with the cold margarine. Place salmon in dish. Add broth. Season fish with salt, pepper, and dill.

Roast fish for 12 to 15 minutes, until fish flakes easily with a fork.

Shrimp Cocktail

I wasn't prepared for how my boys attacked the shrimp cocktail hors d'oeuvre I had brought home for my husband and myself. So I did what any good mother would do: I let them eat that round and made sure to have more on hand the next time!

1 lb. cooked, shelled, de-veined, chilled shrimp
1 C dairy-free, egg-free, nut-free jarred cocktail sauce for shellfish

Dip and eat for great taste, fun, and nutrition.

Barbequed Salmon

My boys love barbequed salmon. Soy margarine tastes as sweet as dairy butter to us and so this is delectable.

1 (4 to 5 lb.) salmon, cleaned and halved, skin left on
½ C onion, diced
4 cloves garlic, diced
½ C dairy-free margarine, cut into chunks
salt and pepper to taste

Prepare two foil "boats" for the top rack of the grill.

Place each salmon half, skin side down, on the foil.

Divide margarine, onion, and garlic in half and spread over each portion of the fish.

Grill over medium-low heat, with the top closed, until the fish flesh flakes and the juices run opaque (approximately half an hour).

Serve with German Potato Salad (see Side Dishes) and corn-on-the-cob for a sweet summer meal.

Pan Fried Trout

My husband takes the boys fishing and we cook up their catch to their delight.

Trout (cleaned, without head or tail, with the skin left on)
flour--enough to coat all sides of the fish
dairy-free margarine (about 2 Tbl., to taste, per fish)
pepper to taste

Coat both sides of the fish (skin) with flour. Place in a large skillet with chunks of margarine. Fry the fish uncovered over medium heat, turning occasionally, till the meat is flaky.

The males in my house especially enjoy eating the fried skin. My husband picks at the fish and doles out boneless portions until the fish is completely gone and they have more reason to go back out fishing.

Crab Legs

Need I say anything about this "beachy" favorite?? Dip it in melted dairy-free margarine and delight your taste buds.

Crab legs (or the whole crab!); still in the shell
Melted dairy-free margarine

Wash crab legs thoroughly. Cover crab with water in a large pot. Boil in salted water until meat is solid and white and comes out in pieces.

Carefully break into the shell and remove crabmeat. Dip hot, cooked crabmeat into your own personal dipping cup of melted margarine for a dinner or appetizer rich in taste and summertime goodness!

Creamy Tuna Vegetable Noodle

This kid-pleasing noodle dish is creamy, yummy, and fulfilling without using any dairy. Salmon can be used in place of the tuna for a different taste.

½ lb. egg-free elbow pasta
3 tsp. olive oil
1 clove garlic, minced
2 Tbl. flour
2½ C dairy-free chicken broth
cooked veggies: carrots, broccoli, and snow peas (whatever they eat best!)
1 can (6 oz.) water-packed tuna or (7 oz.) canned salmon
¼ tsp. tarragon

Cook pasta according to package directions.

Heat olive oil in a skillet. Add garlic; sauté briefly, then stir in flour. Whisk until well blended.

Gradually add broth. Continue whisking until sauce thickens.

Add cooked vegetables, tuna, and tarragon. Heat through.

Serve over hot, cooked pasta.

Shrimp Shish Kebabs

I think this is our favorite way to eat shrimp. My boys will eat almost a whole skewer each! It is simple to prepare. Serve with steamed broccoli and prepared "safe" herb couscous.

1 lb. shelled, de-veined shrimp
Tex-Mex or Asian Marinade
skewers

Tex-Mex Marinade	**Asian Marinade**
6 tsp. lime juice	6 tsp. soy sauce
3 tsp. garlic, minced	3 tsp. garlic, minced
3 tsp. garlic powder	3 tsp. vegetable oil
3 tsp. vegetable oil	3 tsp. sesame oil

Prepare grill by cleaning it and then coating with dairy-free cooking spray.

Combine the ingredients for your choice of marinade in a large, Ziploc bag. Shell and de-vein shrimp, if necessary. Add shrimp to the bag, and seal. Turn the bag until the meat is coated evenly and then place in the refrigerator for five to ten minutes. Preheat the grill while the meat is marinating.

Remove the shrimp from the bag, and discard any leftover marinade. Using metal skewers, thread the shrimp onto the skewers.

Grill the kebabs over medium-high heat for about four minutes per side, or until the shrimp turns pink and is cooked through. Remove the kebabs from the skewers with a fork and serve.

Teriyaki Shrimp/Scallop Kebabs

This delicious thick glaze clings to the seafood when you grill it, giving the meat a great flavor. You can use it for chicken, beef, or pork as well. Serve it with a cold Yakisoba noodle salad (see below) and a vegetable for a great meal.

Teriyaki glaze:
1½ tsp. cornstarch
1½ tsp. water
¼ C soy sauce
3 Tbl. brown sugar
1½ Tbl. rice vinegar
1 tsp. ground ginger
¼ tsp. crushed red pepper
1 clove garlic, minced
1 to 1½ lbs. shrimp, shelled and de-veined

Whisk together the cornstarch and water until smooth; add to a small saucepan. Add soy sauce, brown sugar, rice vinegar, ginger, red pepper, and garlic. Bring to a boil over medium-high heat. Cook for an additional 2 minutes, until thickened. Cool.

Thread shrimp onto skewers. Brush seafood with some olive oil and place on grill that has been coated with dairy-free cooking spray. Cook for about 3 minutes. Turn the kebabs and brush with half of the teriyaki glaze. Turn once more and brush with remaining glaze. Cook until shrimp is pink and firm.

Yakisoba noodles: rinse a 1 lb. bag of noodles in warm water to separate. Toss with a couple of tablespoons of orange juice, a dash of sesame oil, a touch of soy sauce, and chopped green onions. Chill in the refrigerator until served.

Easy Oven Fish

I tried this dish because I was trying to incorporate more fish into our diets and it fit our needs. The boys loved it and asked for more!

1 lb. (6 to 8 ounce fillets) boneless, skinless white fish (we like flounder or cod)
1 tomato, diced
basil
lemon juice (fresh is best)
olive oil
Foil

Preheat oven to 400 degrees.

Cut 8-inch pieces of foil for each fillet of fish. Place one fillet in the center of the foil. Sprinkle diced tomatoes and basil on top of the fish. Squeeze a dash of lemon and drizzle a splash of olive oil over each fillet. Gather the ends of the foil over the center and seal, creating individual foil packets.

Place each foil packet on a cookie sheet and bake for 10 to 12 minutes.

Open carefully and serve immediately.

DINNERS WITH TOFU

Tofu Stir Fry

The sesame oil in this dish lends such a wonderful flavor and aroma to this loved dinner. The tofu gets nice and crunchy with this preparation.

1 (1 lb.) boxed extra-firm tofu
1 head of broccoli, diced
1 sweet red pepper, cut into ½ -inch strips
½ sweet or red onion, cut into ½ -inch strips
1 cup sliced mushrooms
2 Tbl. sesame oil
hot cooked rice

Chop the tofu into small, bite-sized pieces. Sauté the tofu in a large skillet or Dutch oven in the sesame oil for about 20 minutes, stirring constantly. Chop the vegetables.

Add the vegetables to the tofu in the pan and continue sautéing until vegetables are crisp tender.

Serve over hot rice with sweet and sour sauce.

Sweet and Sour Sauce:
½ C packed brown sugar
1 Tbl. cornstarch
1/3 C red wine vinegar
1/3 C unsweetened pineapple juice
1 Tbl. soy sauce
¼ tsp. garlic powder
¼ tsp. ground ginger

In a 2-cup glass-measuring cup, combine all ingredients. Cook in the microwave, uncovered, on 100% power (high) for 3 to 5 minutes or till thickened and bubbly, stirring every minute till mixture starts to thicken, then every 30 seconds. Cook 30 seconds more.

Tofu Indonesian-Style

"More tofu please!" accompanies this dish at dinner. This fabulous, flavorful dish gets your kids to easily eat tofu. The Soy Nut Butter taste is enriched with a variety of subtle spices. Simple to prepare and simply delicious!

¼ C Soy Nut Butter (peanut butter substitute, found in the health section)
¼ C soy sauce
¼ C water
½ tsp. sesame oil
½ tsp. ground ginger
1 tsp. rice vinegar
1 Tbl. brown sugar
2 cloves garlic, minced
2 Tbl. nut-free, packaged sesame seeds
3 green onions, sliced thinly
1 (1 lb.) extra-firm tofu
hot cooked rice

Preheat oven to 375 degrees.

Combine the Soy Nut Butter, soy sauce, water, sesame oil, ginger, rice vinegar, and brown sugar in a medium bowl. Whisk until smooth. Mix in garlic, sesame seeds, and green onions.

Spoon ¼ C sauce into an 8-inch baking pan.

Dice tofu and spread evenly in pan on top of sauce. Top with remainder of sauce.

Bake for 25 minutes.

Serve over hot, cooked rice.

Tofu Spaghetti

This is my tried and true (and quick!) spaghetti sauce that my kids crave. My boys love this tofu version on equal terms with its beefy cousin.   I always serve my drop biscuits with this dinner.

1 (1 lb.) package extra-firm tofu
¾ C onion, diced
5 cloves garlic, minced
¾ C zucchini, diced
½ C green or red pepper, diced
1 Tbl. olive oil
1 can (14.5 oz.) diced tomatoes (with juice)
1 can (15 oz.) tomato sauce
1 Bay leaf
1 Tbl. oregano
1 Tbl. basil
1 Tbl. sugar
pasta: prepared according to package directions.

In large skillet or saucepan, sauté tofu, onion, garlic, zucchini, and red/green pepper in the olive oil until tender.

Add diced tomatoes, tomato sauce, bay leaf, oregano, basil, and sugar. Bring to a boil.

Reduce heat; cover, and simmer for at least 20 to 30 minutes; longer simmer times boost a more intense flavor.

Serve over fun, hot noodles, with biscuits on the side.

MISCELLANEOUS
KID PLEASING MAIN MEALS

Slow Cooked Beans

This meal is one of our summer standards. It tastes just like "kid pleasing" sunshine. This recipe is for a large crowd, so I half the recipe if it is just for our family.

2 large cans (3 lbs. 5 oz.) Pork and Beans
1 large can (20 oz.) of pineapple chunks, drained
1 green pepper, diced
1 large onion, diced
½ lb. (dairy-, egg- free) hot dogs or sausages
1 C brown sugar
2 Tbl. prepared, regular mustard
2 Tbl. Worchester sauce
1 Tbl. liquid smoke (found on the spice aisle)
½ C molasses
1 C ketchup

Mix all ingredients in a crock pot, Dutch oven, or extra-large saucepan and simmer, stirring occasionally:

1) on the stovetop at a simmer for 1 to 2 hours, occasionally stirring
2) on Low heat in the crock pot for 3 to 4 hours
3) in a 350-degree oven for 3 to 4 hours, occasionally stirring

Smokey Roll Ups

Leighton named this favorite camping dish. We've been known to skewer some and pop them on the grill for a fun meal at home. Somehow the grilling process makes these little tasty sausages addicting!

1 (1 lb.) package Lit'l Smokies sausages (Always check ingredients to see if they are safe!)
1 package dairy-free, flour tortillas
vegan (dairy-free, egg-free) cheese substitute slices(optional)

Cut tortillas into 2-inch strips. Cut vegan cheese slices into 2-inch strips.

Place a cheese strip and a Little Smokey at end of a tortilla strip and roll up; skewer on a metal rod through the middle of the roll.

Roast over a fire, lay on a grill, or sauté (without the skewers) in olive oil in a large skillet until the tortilla roll is nicely browned and crispy.

Eat as is, or dip in dairy-free, nut-free barbeque sauce.

Kingma Korn Puppies

Here is a delicious, fun dish that will be requested at your table for years!

1 C flour
¾ C corn meal
1/3 C sugar
1 Tbl. baking powder
½ tsp. salt
1 tsp. chili powder
1 tsp. cumin
1 tsp. garlic powder
1 C plain soymilk
2 Tbl. vegetable oil
1½ Tbl. water, 1½ Tbl. oil, 1 tsp. baking powder; mixed together
3 or 4 dairy-free hot dogs, cut into 1-inch pieces.

Preheat oven to 400 degrees. Grease mini-muffin tin (x24 sections).

Whisk together flour, corn meal, sugar, baking powder, salt, chili powder, cumin, and garlic powder in a large bowl. Set aside.

Combine soymilk, water/oil/baking powder mixture, and oil in a separate bowl.

Add wet ingredients to dry ingredients. Stir just until blended.

Fill each mini-muffin section half full with batter. Place a hot dog piece into each. Then add enough batter to each section to cover the hot dog.

Bake 10 to 12 minutes, until golden brown and tester comes out clean.

Cool slightly before removing. Serve warm with ketchup and mustard.

Pizza

Pizza with extra cheese was the hardest thing to give up for my husband. I have never felt safe ordering any pizza from an establishment and thus went on a quest to find a suitable replacement that I could prepare at home. I really concentrate on preparing a great crust, a sweet sauce, and then filling it up with yummy allowed meat.

Pizza sauce:
½ C onion, finely diced
1 (15 oz.) can tomato sauce
1 (15 oz.) can diced tomatoes
2 Tbl. basil
2 tsp. sugar
2 tsp. oregano
2 cloves garlic, minced
¾ tsp. pepper

Sauté onion, in a medium saucepan, in a dash of olive oil until soft. Add the rest of ingredients to the onions in the saucepan. Bring to a boil. Reduce heat; cover and simmer about 10 minutes.

Pizza crust:
2¾ C flour
1 package (2¼ tsp) active dry yeast
¼ tsp. salt
1 C warm water (120 to 130 degrees)
2 Tbl. vegetable oil
corn meal

In a large bowl whisk together 1¼ C flour, yeast and salt. Add warm water and oil. Beat well, scraping bowl constantly. Using a spoon, stir in as much of the remaining flour as you can. In the bowl, knead in enough remaining flour to make moderately stiff dough that is smooth and elastic (knead 6 to 8 minutes total). Cover and let rest 10 minutes.

Preheat oven to 425 degrees. Grease a large pizza pan with dairy-free cooking spray and sprinkle with corn meal, shaking over the sink to remove the excess corn meal.

On a lightly floured surface, roll dough into a 16-inch circle. Transfer to the pan. Build up edges slightly. Prick crust with fork. Do not let rise. Bake for about 12 minutes, or until browned.

Lower oven temperature to 350 degrees. Spread Pizza Sauce over hot crust. Sprinkle meat and vegetables over the top. Bake 10 to 15 minutes more, or until toppings are hot.

OR use dairy-free, egg-free, nut-free English Muffins for the crust: "Mini-Pizzas!"

Pizza Toppings (check meat ingredients EVERY time!):
Mild Italian Sausage (ground), use a whole pound for a meaty meal: just brown in a skillet and drain
Pepperoni
Canadian Bacon
sliced olives
red pepper strips
pineapple (cut into small chunks/crushed)
zucchini/mushrooms/onions (okay--maybe just on the parent's side)

For a nice, tasty different meal, try a different topping:

Spicy Ground Beef Pizza Topping
¾ lb. ground beef
1 C onion, finely diced
¼ C green pepper, finely diced
1 (14.5-oz.) can diced tomatoes
1 Tbl. dried parsley
1 clove garlic, minced
¼ tsp. cumin
¼ tsp. coriander
1/8 tsp. allspice
pepper to taste

Brown beef in skillet. Drain fat. Add remaining ingredients and simmer, covered, about 20 minutes. Spread topping on pizza crust and bake 15 minutes.

Pancakes

These pancakes are light, fluffy, and tasty. No one will know they lack eggs and dairy. These have a great texture and taste.

2 C flour
2 Tbl. sugar
4 tsp. baking powder
½ tsp. salt
1½ Tbl. water, 1½ Tbl. oil, 1 tsp. baking powder; mixed together
2 C soymilk (plain or vanilla)
4 Tbl. vegetable oil
1½ tsp. vanilla

In a large bowl whisk together flour, sugar, baking powder, and salt. Set aside.

In a separate bowl, combine water/oil/baking powder mixture, soymilk, oil, and vanilla.

Add wet ingredients to dry ingredients and stir just until blended, but still lumpy.

Cook on a hot griddle coated with dairy-free cooking spray until golden brown on each side.

Top with Breakfast Citrus Sauce (see Miscellaneous Meals).

I often reduce the amount of unbleached flour and add the equivalent in wheat bran, whole-wheat flour, or ground-up flaxseed for extra nutrition.

Waffles

This breakfast staple is thick, yet light. The vanilla really gives the waffles a boost in flavor and texture.

3½ C flour
2 Tbl. baking powder
½ tsp. salt
1½ Tbl. water, 1½ Tbl. oil, 1 tsp. baking powder; mixed together
3½ C soymilk (plain or vanilla)
1 C vegetable oil
1½ tsp. vanilla
dairy-free cooking spray

Whisk together flour, baking powder, and salt; set aside.

In a separate bowl, combine water/oil/baking powder mixture, soymilk, oil, and vanilla.

Add wet ingredients to dry ingredients and stir just until blended, but still lumpy.

Pour 3/4 to 1 cup batter onto grids of a preheated, lightly greased waffle baker. Bake according to manufacturer's directions.

*Again, I like to substitute some wheat germ or wheat bran, for the regular flour, to the mixture for a fiber boost.

Fettuccini Alfredo

Yes—this yummy dish is comparable to the real thing. My kids aren't too hot about the traditional thick noodles, so I usually just prepare regular spaghetti noodles instead.

2 (15-ounce) cans Great Northern White beans
¾ to 1 C plain soymilk (to your preference)
1 Tbl. jarred roasted garlic (or to taste)
dash of salt
¼ tsp. freshly ground black pepper
¼ tsp. freshly ground nutmeg
cooked broccoli—as much as your kids will eat!
cooked dairy-free, egg-free pasta: fettuccini or spaghetti

Puree half of the beans with half of the soymilk (go crazy with the blender and make sure all of the bean casings get pulverized); pour into large saucepan. Repeat with the remaining beans and soymilk. Measure the soymilk to your thickness preference.

Add roasted garlic, salt, pepper, nutmeg, and broccoli and simmer for 15 to 20 minutes. Grinding your own nutmeg really adds a wonderful flavor. I bought a jar of nutmeg nuts and just grate it on the small holes on my grater.

Serve over hot, cooked noodles.

**I include this recipe as a vegetarian meal, but I must admit my boys like it better when I add sautéed chicken chunks (I brown the chicken in margarine or olive oil, then add the broccoli, sautéing until the chicken is no longer pink in the middle and the broccoli is tender).

Breakfast Citrus Sauce

My whole family goes crazy for this "delish" topping for
pancakes and waffles. It tastes sunny, happy, and tropical.
This is our number one topping for pancakes.

¼ C sugar
1 Tbl. cornstarch
1¼ C orange juice
2 tsp. dairy-free margarine, cut into chunks
1 (8 oz. can) crushed pineapple
1 banana, sliced

Combine sugar and cornstarch in a small saucepan. Whisk in
orange juice.

Cook over medium heat until thick, stirring, with a wooden
spoon, constantly. Cook and stir an additional two minutes.

Remove from heat and stir in margarine and pineapple.

After the mixture has cooled a bit, add sliced bananas and
serve warm over pancakes or waffles.

Special Occasion Apple Pancakes

These incredibly tasty pancakes will be repeatedly requested at your house!

1 C flour
1 tsp. baking powder
½ tsp. baking soda
1 tsp. cinnamon
¼ tsp. salt
1 C soymilk: plain or vanilla
2 Tbl. oil
1½ Tbl. water, 1½ Tbl. oil, 1 tsp. baking powder; mixed together
1 apple: cored, peeled, and thinly sliced
dairy-free margarine

In a large bowl, whisk together flour, baking powder, baking soda, cinnamon, and salt. Set aside.

In a separate bowl, combine soymilk, oil, and water/oil/baking powder mixture.

Add the wet ingredients to the dry ingredients and stir until smooth. Add the sliced apples and stir to combine.

Fry pancakes in dairy-free margarine until cooked in the middle. Make sure there are apple slices in each pancake.

Serve with syrup or sweet cream: ½ C soy sour cream mixed with 1½ Tbl. brown sugar.

Play Dough

Evan is a play dough maniac and I thought I would include the BEST recipe for play dough that will ensure you a good hour of quiet time if you make it for your child.

1 C flour
½ C salt
2 tsp. cream of tartar
1 C water
1 Tbl. oil
drops of food coloring

In a large, nonstick pan whisk together the flour, salt, and cream of tartar. Add water, oil, and preferred food coloring and mix well.

Cook over medium heat, stirring with a wooden spoon, for about three minutes, or until mixture pulls away from pan.

Knead dough immediately until desired consistency. Store in an airtight container.

SUPER QUICK MEALS FOR TIRED MOTHERS

Okay--this isn't the fancy culinary section, but the section that gets the job quickly done WITHOUT eggs or dairy. You can't order pizza, cheese omelets are out, there is nothing in the freezer, what do you prepare tonight in less than an hour when you are tired and sick of cooking? We are not supposed to be martyrs all the time and we mothers of children allergic to dairy and eggs deserve easy food too! Here are forty-two menus that you can easily and quickly prepare.

Menu One
Hamburgers-- shaped from hand and grilled on the George Forman Grill (or fried on the skillet), with "safe" buns or "safe" bagels
Tater Tots--(or homemade fries)-- in the oven
Canned sweet peas--on the stovetop
Tots/Fries: Slice potatoes into ½- x ½- x 4- inch strips; place into a large Zip Lock bag. Spray cooking oil into the bag and a large dash of paprika, shake well and bake at 425 degrees till crispy.

Menu Two
All beef sausages-- boiled on the stovetop, with "safe" buns
"Veggie" surprise-- Top Ramen noodles, boiled with frozen mixed vegetables (always check the spice packet ingredients for dairy!). Okay--I confess, this is one of my kids' all time favorite meals. They eat a lot of vegetables that are stuck to the ramen noodles, so I just concentrate on what a good mother I am for getting them to eat so many vegetables!

Menu Three
Honey Mustard Chicken--mix mustard and honey in equal measures and pour on top of chicken breasts; bake at 350 degrees for an hour
Baked potatoes--bake at 350 degrees for an hour, top with dairy-free margarine and chives from the garden
Broccoli--steamed on the stovetop

Menu four

Spaghetti--Add about 2 tsp. each (to taste) of: garlic powder, onion powder, basil, oregano, and sugar to one can of tomato sauce and one can of diced tomatoes for sauce. Add a small container of tofu, diced. Serve over hot pasta. Canned sweet corn-- on the stovetop

Garlic bread--smear some dairy-free margarine on a slice of "safe" bread and sprinkle some garlic salt on top. Bake in a 350 degree oven for about 5 minutes, or till browned.

Menu Five

Rice a Roni package mix with Chicken and Vegetables-- Sauté bite-sized pieces of chicken and vegetables in the dairy-free margarine before you add the rice and roni. Then prepare as directed. (Always check the ingredients: some spice packets have dairy in them!).

Menu Six

Grilled Chicken breasts-- on the BBQ with "safe" BBQ sauce
Creamy Noodles --(see Side Dishes)
Corn on the cob-- boiled on the stovetop

Menu Seven

Pork Chops-- with a pat of dairy-free margarine and some seasonings sprinkled on top, baked in oven for 1 hour
Baked potato — in oven for 1 hour
Frozen mixed vegetables-- boiled on stovetop

Menu Eight

Hash Browns-- grate some potatoes, chop some vegetables (onion, mushrooms, green/red pepper, etc.), and add some cooked, chopped ham. Cook with some olive oil in a large skillet on the stovetop, stirring constantly.
Homemade "safe" toast-- on the side

Menu Nine

Kingma Korn Puppies (see Miscellaneous Main Meals)
Frozen corn –boiled on the stovetop

Menu Ten
Chilidogs-- make with "safe" canned chili and dairy-free, all-beef sausages on "safe" open buns
Brown-sugar carrots-- (see recipe in Side Dishes)

Menu Eleven
Steak Strips-- sauté steak strips in skillet with sesame oil
Aunt Jean's Rice-- (see Side Dishes)
Broccoli—steamed on the stovetop

Menu Twelve
Sloppy Joes-- ground 1 lb. beef, add 1C diced onion, ½C diced green pepper, ¾C "safe" BBQ sauce, and 3 Tbl. Ketchup; cook till well combined and the flavors seep together. Serve on "safe" buns.
Sweet corn—on the stovetop

Menu Thirteen
French Dip hot sandwiches-- warm "safe" roast beef slices and "safe" buns smeared with dairy-free margarine in oven. Prepare au jus by boiling 2 dairy-free "safe" beef bouillon cubes per 1 C water
Tater tots/fries-- in the oven
Fresh green beans-- boiled on the stovetop

Menu Fourteen
Smokey Roll-Ups- (see recipe in Miscellaneous Main Meals)
Aunt Jean's Rice—(see Side Dishes)
Canned sweet peas—on the stovetop

Menu Fifteen
Pepperoni Roll-Ups-- (see recipe in Snacks)
Canned Tomato soup—on the stovetop

Menu Sixteen
Lemon Chicken Sauté--(see recipe Dinners with Chicken)
Creamy Noodles—(see Side Dishes)
Fresh green beans-- steamed on the stovetop

Menu Seventeen
Pancakes or Waffles-- (with lots of wheat bran folded in)
Applesauce-- jarred or canned
Sausages-- fried in a skillet (Breakfast for dinner is always fun!)

Menu Eighteen
Mandarin Chicken--(see Dinners with Chicken)
Broccoli—steamed on the stovetop

Menu Nineteen
Shrimp or Chicken Shish Kebabs--(see Dinners with Seafood or Chicken)
Sautéed turnips--(see recipe in Side Dishes)
Corn on the cob-- boiled on the stovetop

Menu Twenty
Tofu Indonesian Style--(see Dinners with Tofu)
Hot Rice
Broccoli-- steamed on the stovetop

Menu Twenty-one
Beef tacos--made with browned ground beef, canned refried black beans, diced tomatoes, shredded lettuce, and grated carrots, on hard or soft dairy-free shells

Menu Twenty-two
Potato Soup--(see Soups, add some frozen corn to the soup)
Biscuits--(see Baked goods)

Menu Twenty-three
Chicken Stir Fry--(see Dinners with Chicken)--using frozen vegetables (try a frozen package of stir fry vegetables, note: water chestnuts are not nuts!)
Hot rice

Menu Twenty-four
Chicken Nuggets--(see Dinners with Chicken)
Rice-a-Roni--prepared according to package directions
Canned corn--on the stovetop

Menu Twenty-five
Steak--coated with kosher salt and broiled in the oven or grilled outside, until your preferred doneness, with "safe" BBQ sauce
Noodles--(dried, egg-free, dairy-free, boiled according to package directions) served with sea salt and dairy-free margarine
Brown sugar carrots—(see Side Dishes)

Menu Twenty-six
Mini pizzas--
Sauce: bring ½ (14.5 oz.) can tomato sauce, ½ (15 oz.) can diced tomatoes, dash of garlic powder, dash of onion powder, 1 Tbl. basil, 1 tsp. sugar, 1 tsp. oregano to a boil. Reduce heat and simmer for 5 minutes.

Crust—use toasted "safe" English muffins or "safe" bagels
Toppings-- pepperoni, sliced olives

Top muffins with sauce and toppings, heat thoroughly in 350 degree oven.

Menu Twenty-seven
Teriyaki chicken or shrimp--(see appropriate dinners), grilled on BBQ
Yakisoba noodles--rinse noodles in warm water to separate. Toss with some orange juice, sesame oil, a touch of soy sauce, and chopped green onions.
Broccoli--steamed on the stovetop.

Menu Twenty-eight
Fettuccini Alfredo with Chicken and Broccoli--(see Miscellaneous Main Meals)

Menu Twenty-nine
Tofu Burgers--we have tried a couple of mixes that you add to tofu; use with "safe" buns, bagels, or bread with the favored condiments.
French Fries--Slice potatoes into ½-x ½- x 4- inch strips; place into a large Zip Lock bag. Spray cooking oil into the bag and a large dash of paprika, shake well and bake at 425 degrees till crispy.
Corn—any style

Menu Thirty
Chicken Strips—breasts sliced into 1-inch slices and quick marinated (15 minutes) in: 1 Tbl. lemon juice, 1½ tsp. grated fresh ginger, ½ tsp. ground black pepper, 2 diced garlic cloves. Cook in large nonstick skillet, generously coated with cooking spray, turning occasionally until no longer pink in the middle. Have "safe" BBQ sauce for dipping.
Couscous--prepared according to manufacturer's directions
Green beans-- steamed on the stovetop

Menu Thirty-one
Chili Mac--(see Dinners with Beef)
Corn-- add some canned corn to mixture in the final stage

Menu Thirty-two
Shrimp and Pasta--(see Dinners with Seafood)
Broccoli--steamed on the stovetop

Menu Thirty-three
Bean Burritos--smear 2 tablespoons of "safe" canned refried beans on the bottom of a tortilla, top with vegan cheese. Roll up burrito style and heat in the microwave with some salsa served on the side.
Mixed vegetables--boiled on the stovetop

Menu Thirty-four
Creamed Pork on Toast Points--(see Dinners with Pork)
Green beans--steamed on the stovetop

Menu Thirty-five
Chicken Paprikash Potatoes--(see Dinners with Chicken)
Corn--frozen, boiled on stovetop

Menu Thirty-six
Poached Salmon--(see Dinners with Seafood)
Noodles--served with dairy-free margarine and a sprinkle of sea-salt
Broccoli--steamed on the stovetop

Menu Thirty-seven
Easy Oven Fish--(see Dinners with Seafood)
Couscous--prepared according to package directions on the stovetop
Cauliflower--steamed on the stovetop

Menu Thirty-eight
Flank steak--(see Dinners with Beef)
Baking Potatoes--use small-sized potatoes, baked with metal poker for quick baking time
Green peas--frozen, boiled on stovetop

Menu Thirty-nine
Creamy Tuna Vegetable Noodle--(see Dinners with Seafood)

Menu Forty
Spanish Rice with Chicken and Beans--(see Side Dishes)

Menu Forty-one
Tarragon Chicken Bun Boats--(see Dinners with Chicken)
Green beans--steamed on the stovetop

Menu Forty-two
Chicken Mole--(see Dinners with Chicken), add frozen corn to the cooking mixture for a complete meal
Hot Rice (optional)
Tortillas--for rolling up the Mole

VEGAN MEALS

I am trying to incorporate at least one meal each week without meat and that means a vegan meal for us. I am in ever search of a meatless meal that appeals to my kids' palettes. The following meals are tried and true in my house.

Menu One
Tofu Indonesian Style--(see Dinners with Tofu) -this is one of the most popular vegan meals in our house.
Hot cooked rice
Steamed broccoli--on the stovetop

Menu Two
Tofu Burgers-- we have tried a couple of mixes that you add to tofu; use with "safe" buns, bagels, or bread.
French Fries-- Slice potatoes into ½- x ½- x 4- inch strips, place into a large Ziploc bag. Spray cooking oil into the bag and a large dash of paprika, shake well and bake at 425 degrees till crispy.
Corn--any style

Menu Three
Tofu Spaghetti--(see Dinners with Tofu) -my boys love this dish on equal terms with its beefy cousin.
Biscuits--(see Muffins& Breads)

Menu Four
Bean enchiladas--(see "Chicken Enchiladas" in Dinners with Chicken), but replace the chicken with a can (15 ounce) of Refried Beans. Delicious!

Menu Five
Slow Cooked Beans--(see Miscellaneous Main Meals), except omit the meat (you won't miss it). Adding tofu is optional.

Menu Six
Spanish Rice--(see Side Dishes). Add black beans and diced zucchini to make a one-dish meal.

Menu Seven
Tofu Stir Fry-- (see Dinners with Tofu)
Hot cooked rice
Sweet and Sour Sauce--(see Stir Fry Chicken in Dinners with Chicken)

Menu Eight
Fettuccine Alfredo--(see Miscellaneous Main Meals)
Hot cooked linguine
Broccoli--steamed on the stovetop

Menu Nine
Baked Potato Soup--(see Soups). Omit the bacon, and sauté the onions and garlic in olive oil instead. Add additional cooked vegetables for variety. Use all-vegetable broth in place of the chicken broth.
Fresh homemade bread--from the bread machine.

Menu Ten
Split Pea Soup--(see Soups). Omit the cooked ham and add a variety of cooked vegetables for variety. Use all-vegetable broth instead of chicken broth.
Fresh homemade bread--from the bread machine

Menu Eleven
Beans and Rice--Use vegetable broth instead of water and add diced onion and minced garlic to the liquid when cooking dried beans (following package directions). Roll the beans and rice up in a tortilla with a dash of salsa and dip into soy sour cream substitute.
Hot cooked rice--made with soy-margarine.
Dairy-free flour tortillas--with salsa on the side

Menu Twelve
Bean Burritos--smear 2 tablespoons of "safe" canned vegetarian refried beans on the bottom of a "safe" tortilla, top with vegan cheese. Roll up burrito style and heat in the microwave with some salsa served on the side.
Mixed vegetables--boiled on the stovetop

SOUPS

Split Pea Soup

Is there anything as satisfying as a bowl of warm, thick pea soup chock full of veggies and ham? My kids have always requested this recipe. Set up your bread machine that morning and you are set up for a real meal.   This yummy soup is surprisingly simple to prepare.

3 C dry split peas (rinsed and sorted)
about 7 C of water (more as needed)
1 bay leaf
2 tsp. salt
½ to 1 tsp. dry mustard (to taste)
1 C onion, minced
4 to 5 cloves garlic, minced
3 medium carrots, chopped
2 medium potatoes, chopped small
1 lb. cooked, chopped ham
black pepper
3 to 4 Tbl. red wine vinegar (to taste)

Place prepared split peas, water, bay leaf, salt, and dry mustard in a Dutch oven or large capacity saucepan. Bring to a boil, lower heat and simmer, partially covered, for about 20 minutes.

Add vegetables and ham. Partially cover, and simmer for an additional 40 minutes with occasional stirring. Add some water if necessary.

Add black pepper and vinegar to taste.

Baked Potato Soup

This soup is delicious. The crispy skin topping adds a potato chip element that the kids can't resist.

4 large baking potatoes
1 lb. bacon
3/4 C onion, diced
3 cloves garlic, minced
¼ C flour
3 C dairy-free, egg-free chicken broth
olive oil for brushing the potato skin strips

After scrubbing the potatoes and pricking them with a fork, bake in a 350 degree oven for 75 to 80 minutes, or until an inserted fork ensures "mashability."

Let potatoes cool to room temperature. Cut each in half, lengthwise, and scoop out the insides into a large bowl. Pile up the skins on a plate; set aside.

Cook bacon in a Dutch oven or large skillet until lightly browned, but with no burn spots in the pan; remove to a plate covered with a paper towel. Remove all but one tablespoon of bacon grease in pan.

Sauté onions and garlic in the 1 Tbl. reserved bacon grease until tender. Add flour and mix well. Add 2 cups of chicken broth all at once; mix well.

Mash the potatoes with a hand masher; add to the pan. Add additional chicken broth to desired consistency. Use hand masher to mash any remaining lumps. Simmer on stovetop.

Meanwhile, cover bacon with additional paper towel(s) and microwave on HIGH until crispy--about 3 minutes; check after each minute. Let cool slightly. Crumble bacon into soup and simmer for about 10 to 15 minutes, or until flavors meld.

Cut reserved, cool potato skins into ½ -inch strips. Brush each side with olive oil. Arrange in a single layer on cookie sheet. Broil until crispy--about 3 minutes.

Serve soup in bowls garnished with skin strips.

Cream of Mushroom Soup

Here is a recipe to use as a "safe" substitution for those traditional kid-friendly meals that you know and love. Stock up on mushrooms when they are in season and triple the recipe, freeze flat in desired-size Ziploc bags and it can be used instead of the "unsafe" cans.

5 C sliced fresh mushrooms, thoroughly cooked
1½ C dairy-free, egg-free chicken broth
1 Tbl. dairy-free margarine
1 Tbl. flour
1/8 tsp. dried thyme
1/8 tsp. salt
dash pepper
1 C plain soymilk

In a blender or food processor, combine the cooked mushrooms and 3/4 C of the chicken broth. Cover and process about 1 minute, or until smooth. Set aside.

In a medium saucepan melt margarine. Stir in flour, thyme, salt, and pepper. Add plain soymilk all at once. Cook and stir until slightly thickened and bubbly. Cook 1 minute more.

Stir in pureed vegetable mixture and remaining ¾C broth. Cook and stir until heated through.

Use it for your cooking cream needs.

Chicken Tortilla Soup

This soup tastes and looks like a million bucks! You don't know it's a naturally dairy- and egg- free soup. I've received rave reviews from adults and kids alike. It is a meal in itself. AND--it is very easy to prepare!

1/3 C onion, diced
3 cloves garlic, minced
¾ tsp. cumin
¾ tsp. oregano
¼ tsp. chili powder
¼ tsp. pepper
8 C dairy-free chicken broth
1 can (14 oz) diced tomatoes, with juice
1 can (4 oz) diced green chilies
10 dairy-free corn tortillas (6 in. wide)
1½ lb. boneless, skinless chicken breast

In Dutch oven or large saucepan over medium heat, stir onion, garlic, cumin, oregano, chili powder, and pepper until spices are fragrant, about 1 minute. Add broth, tomatoes (with juice), and green chilies. Cover and bring to a boil over high heat.

Meanwhile, stack tortillas and cut into 1/8-inch wide strips. Add to boiling broth. Reduce heat, cover, and simmer for 15 minutes, stirring occasionally.

Rinse chicken and cut into ½-inch pieces.

Add chicken to broth and return to a boil over high heat. Reduce heat, cover, and simmer until chicken is white in center (cut to test), about 5 minutes.

Chicken Confetti Soup

This soup is SO delicious! It tastes exotic with the coconut milk and crisp, fresh vegetables and is very healthy.

1 lb. skinless, boneless chicken breasts, cut into 1-inch cubes
2 Tbl. vegetable oil (divided)
8 cloves garlic, minced
4 tsp. minced fresh ginger
1/8 tsp. red pepper flakes
1 tsp. ground cumin
4 C water
1 (14-oz.) can unsweetened coconut milk
2 C shredded carrots
2 C broccoli florets, chopped small
1 medium red pepper, cut into bite-sized strips
2 (3-oz.) pkgs. chicken-flavored (dairy-free, egg-free) ramen noodles, coarsely broken
2 C snow pea pods
2 Tbl. soy sauce
4 tsp. lime juice
1 C fresh basil, cut into thin strips
1/3 C snipped fresh cilantro

In a Dutch oven or large capacity saucepan, cook chicken in 1 Tbl. of the oil over medium-high heat for 3 to 4 minutes or until no longer pink and lightly browned. Remove; set aside.

Add remaining oil to pan. Add garlic, ginger, red pepper flakes, and cumin; cook and stir for 30 seconds. Stir in water, coconut milk, carrot, broccoli, red pepper, and noodles (set seasoning packets aside for later). Bring to boiling; reduce heat. Simmer, covered, for 3 minutes.

Stir in cooked chicken, pea pods, contents of seasoning packets, soy sauce and limejuice; then stir in the basil and cilantro.

Quick Potato Soup

This is a hearty, thick, stick-to-your-ribs soup that cooks up almost as fast as heating up a can!

1 lb. bacon or dairy-free sausages
2 large potatoes (peeled and chopped)
2 C dairy-free, egg-free chicken broth
water as needed
onion and garlic to taste; diced

Brown bacon or sausages in a Dutch oven or large saucepan, until there are good brown droppings. Remove meat and cook till crisp in microwave (covered with a paper towel).

Add potatoes to pan. Add chicken broth to pan, and then add enough water to cover the potatoes. Boil 10 minutes, or until potatoes come apart. Meanwhile, sauté onions and garlic in 1 Tbl. olive oil in a separate pan.

Add cooked meat and sautéed garlic and onion mixture to soup.

Blend with a hand blender, in pan, till smooth.

SIDE DISHES

"Aunt Jean's" Rice

This recipe comes from a dear neighbor of mine before the allergy situation arose. It originally was topped with shredded cheddar and sliced almonds. But it is still our family's favorite rice dish, even without the old topping. I have received RAVE reviews for this dish. It is excellent for potlucks. My husband loves it for lunch the next day. We now have to double the recipe, to make sure everybody gets his or her fill.

½ onion, diced
¼ C dairy-free margarine
1 can (10 ¼ -oz.) dairy-free, egg-free beef broth (double strength), or make your own by using two bouillon cubes and 10 ounces of boiling water
1 can (4-oz.) mushrooms with juice
1 C uncooked rice

Preheat oven to 350 degrees.

Sauté onions in margarine in large saucepan. Add beef broth, 1/3 can (or 3 ounces) water, mushrooms, and rice. Bring to a boil. Boil one minute, stirring occasionally. Remove from heat.

Place mixture in a casserole dish and bake uncovered for 20 minutes.

Creamy Noodles

These noodles are creamy and yummy. My kids can't get enough of this dish! AND--it's simple to prepare!

1 C plain soymilk
1 C water
1 dairy-free, egg-free chicken bouillon cube
1 Tbl. dairy-free margarine
1¼ C egg-free elbow macaroni
dash of garlic powder
dash of basil

Bring plain soymilk, water, bouillon, and margarine to a boil in a medium saucepan over medium-high heat.

Add noodles and spices.

Reduce heat and simmer, uncovered, stirring occasionally. Most of the liquid will be absorbed by the noodles, creating a creamy consistency.

Turnip Sauté

A tasty alternative to fried potatoes and/or a new way to serve a vegetable on your dinner table, Turnip Sauté will be a winner.

2 to 3 medium turnips
olive oil
dash of salt and pepper

Peel and thinly slice the turnips. Sauté slices in olive oil in a large skillet, turning constantly. Lightly season with salt and pepper. Serve warm.

Use ketchup or dairy-free, egg-free barbeque sauce for dipping.

Brown-Sugar Carrots

When I prepare carrots in either of the following two ways, I'm guaranteed that my kids will eat their full quota of vegetables for the day. I double the recipe because they will keep eating these carrots until they are gone.

¾ lb. carrots, peeled and thinly sliced
1 Tbl. dairy-free margarine
1 Tbl. brown sugar

Boil carrots in a small amount of water (barely covering carrots) for 8 to 10 minutes, or until crisp-tender. Drain vegetables; remove from pan. Set aside.

In the same saucepan, combine margarine, brown sugar and dash of salt. Stir over medium heat until combined. Add cooked carrots. Cook, uncovered, for about 2 minutes, or until glazed, stirring frequently.

Honey Carrots

3 Tbl. dairy-free margarine
4 C carrots, thinly sliced
3 Tbl. orange juice
¼ tsp. ground ginger
4 Tbl. honey

Combine all ingredients in a saucepan and cover. Cook over low heat for 30 minutes, or until tender. Stir occasionally.

Broccoli Strudel

My kids love broccoli and this is a fun and fancy way to serve the green. It is a great side dish to a nice meal and company raves about it.

1 Tbl. olive oil
1 C onion, diced
1 large bunch broccoli, finely chopped
½ tsp. salt
pepper to taste
2 cloves garlic, minced
2 C homemade breadcrumbs
2 Tbl. lemon juice (fresh is best)
15 sheets dairy-free, egg-free, nut-free filo pastry
3 to 4 Tbl. olive oil for brushing

Reminder: it takes about an hour to thaw out the filo pastry by setting it out on the counter, wrapped in a damp dishtowel. You want it thoroughly thawed for best results.

Preheat oven to 375 degrees. Grease a baking sheet.

Heat 1 Tbl. olive oil in a large skillet. Add onion, and sauté for about 5 minutes over medium heat.

Add broccoli, salt, and pepper, and cook, stirring, for about 5 more minutes. Add garlic, and sauté until the broccoli is just tender (about 5 more minutes). Remove from heat. Stir in breadcrumbs and lemon juice.

TO ASSEMBLE:
Place one sheet of filo pastry on a clean, dry surface. Brush the top lightly with olive oil, and then add another sheet. Brush with oil, and then add another. Continue until you have a pile of 5 filo sheets. Add a third of the filling (at the narrow end), fold in the sides, and gently roll until you have a neat little log (like you would roll a burrito). Brush the top with more oil, and then place it on the baking sheet. Repeat this procedure to make the second and third rolls.

Bake 25 to 30 minutes, until golden and crispy. Cut with a serrated knife. Serve warm. It will cool rapidly once you cut it.

German Potato Salad

You may never go back to the mayonnaise variety after eating this delicious potato salad. Naturally dairy- and egg- free, this dish is completely authentic and delicious.

1½ lb. red potatoes
3 slices crispy cooked bacon
1/3 C onion, diced
1 Tbl. flour
1 Tbl. sugar
1 tsp. salt
dash of pepper
1/3 C water
1/6 C white vinegar

Wash and peel potatoes. Fill a large saucepan with enough water to cover the potatoes. Heat water to boiling. Add potatoes. Cover; boil for 30 to 35 minutes, or until tender. Drain; set aside to cool thoroughly.

In a large skillet, fry bacon until crisp; remove and drain all but a tablespoon of bacon drippings. Cook onion in drippings until tender and golden brown. Stir in flour, sugar, salt, and pepper. Cook over low heat, stirring until bubbly. Stir in water and vinegar. Bring to a boil, and then stir constantly for 1 minute.

Remove from heat and let cool completely. Meanwhile cut cooked potatoes into ½- inch chunks.

Combine dressing with the potatoes and serve warm or cool. Enjoy!

Sweet Potato Casserole

This is a perfect side dish to complement the holiday table. It is also a super way to get your kids to eat sweet potatoes, as it tastes like dessert!

2 medium sweet potatoes
¼ C dairy-free margarine, divided
2 Tbl. raisins
1 tsp. grated orange peel
¼ tsp. salt
¼ tsp. ground cinnamon
dash ground nutmeg (to taste)
4 Tbl. flaked, sweetened coconut

Bake or boil sweet potatoes until soft.

Preheat oven to 350 degrees.

Transfer the potatoes to a large bowl and mash well. Stir in 2 Tbl. margarine, raisins, orange peel, salt, cinnamon, and nutmeg until well mixed.

Spread in an 8-inch x 11-inch baking dish.

Melt the remaining 2 Tbl. margarine and toss with the coconut. Sprinkle over the top of the sweet potato mixture.

Bake uncovered for 25 to 30 minutes, until golden.

Crunchy Salad

Finally! A salad that your kids actually eat! This crunchy concoction topped with sweet and tang is a sure addition to your dinner table repertoire.

½ C sugar
½ C vegetable oil
¼ C apple cider vinegar
2 tsp. soy sauce
salt and pepper to taste
2 packages (3 oz.) (dairy-free, egg-free) ramen noodles, broken
4 Tbl. dairy-free margarine
1½ C broccoli, finely chopped
1 small bunch romaine, shredded
4 green onions, thinly sliced

In a salad dressing cruet, combine the sugar, oil, vinegar, soy sauce, salt and pepper; shake well.

Discard seasoning packet from noodles. In a large skillet, sauté noodles in margarine until golden and crunchy, stirring constantly.

In a large salad bowl, combine chopped broccoli, romaine, onions and crunchy noodles. Just before serving, toss with dressing.

Spanish Rice

This rice dish is a great side dish, or a full meal if you add black beans and/or chunks of cooked chicken.

½ C onion, diced
½ C green pepper, diced
1 clove garlic, minced
1 Tbl. vegetable oil
2 (14 oz.) cans diced tomatoes, with juice
3/4 C uncooked rice
1 tsp. sugar
1 tsp. chili powder
1/8 tsp. pepper
dash of hot pepper sauce (to taste/optional)
1 C water

In a Dutch oven or large skillet sauté onion, green pepper, and garlic in oil until tender. Sir in tomatoes with juice, rice, sugar, chili powder, pepper, hot pepper sauce, and water. Bring to boil.

Reduce heat, cover and simmer for 20 to 25 minutes, or until rice is tender and most of the liquid is absorbed.

Option: Add cooked chicken chunks and/or black beans for a one-dish, full meal.

Corn-on-the-Cob Delight

This recipe is a new twist on the usual corn-on-the-cob. The tropical flavor of this corn will have you and your family begging for more!

corn cobs: white or yellow/enough for your family
dairy-free margarine
lime juice
cilantro: rinsed, fresh bunch
foil

Preheat oven to 375 degrees. Get out baking sheet.

Pull out needed number of approximately 8 x 11 -inch foil sheets. Place two corn cobs in the center of each foil sheet. Place each foiled pair onto baking sheet.

Smear a teaspoon of margarine along the top of each cob. Dribble about a teaspoon of lime juice over each cob. Scatter about a teaspoon of fresh cilantro leaves over each corn cob.

Fold and crimp the foil over each pair, creating foil sealed pockets.

Bake in oven 25 to 30 minutes, or until corn is tender.

Remove, open foil pockets, and let cool a bit before serving. You can remove the cilantro leaves.

MUFFINS & BREADS

Orangey Rolls

These are our favorite muffins that are a MUST for Sunday mornings. These are so scrumptious; you'll never make "regular" cinnamon buns again!

Glaze:
½ C cold, dairy-free margarine (divided)
½ C orange juice
½ C sugar
2 tsp. grated orange zest
Rolls:
2 C flour
2 tsp. baking powder
½ tsp. salt
¾ C soymilk—plain or vanilla
1 to 2 Tbl. melted dairy-free margarine, for brushing
cinnamon sugar

Preheat oven to 425 degrees. Grease a 12x muffin tin.

For glaze: Combine ¼ C margarine, orange juice, sugar, and orange zest in a small saucepan. Stir over medium heat until sugar is dissolved; cook for and additional 2 minutes. Pour equal amounts into the muffin compartments.

For rolls: Whisk together flour, baking powder, and salt. Cut in ¼ C margarine with a pastry blender till crumbly.

Add soymilk; stir until dough is formed. Knead briefly in the bowl. Roll out on a well-floured surface into a ¼ inch thick, 8-inch x 12- inch rectangle. Brush with melted margarine, then sprinkle with cinnamon sugar mixture. Roll into a log and crimp edge to close. Cut log into 12 equal slices. Set each piece into muffin tin on top of the glaze.

Bake 18 minutes, or until golden brown. Immediately turn rolls over onto a cooling rack with waxed paper underneath it.

Chocolate Babka

This versatile, delectable treat is perfect for any special occasion. The bread base wonderfully tempers the chocolate delight in the middle. My husband, kids, and company cannot get enough of this dessert bread.

Dough:
1¼ tsp. active dry yeast
¼ C warm water
3 Tbl. dairy-free margarine
½ C soy sour cream substitute (or vanilla soy yogurt)
3 Tbl. sugar
1½ Tbl. water, 1½ Tbl. oil, 1 tsp. baking powder; mixed together
1¼ tsp. salt
2 1/3 C flour

Filling:
5 Tbl. sugar
3 Tbl. unsweetened cocoa powder
2 Tbl. dairy-free margarine, melted
1 C semisweet, dairy-free, nut-free chocolate chips
1 to 2 Tbl. olive oil

Dough: Sprinkle yeast over the warm water in a large, glass bowl. Let stand for 10 minutes.

Meanwhile, in a medium-sized glass bowl melt the margarine. Add soy-sour cream substitute, sugar, water/oil/baking powder mixture, and salt; mix well. Add to the yeast mixture after the ten minutes of standing.

Add flour to the margarine/yeast mixture, one cup at a time, mixing well. Knead in the remaining 1/3 C flour with your hands. Keep dough sticky, soft, and smooth. Spray both the bowl and the top of the dough with non-stick, dairy-free cooking spray. Return the dough to the bowl and cover. Let rise in a warm place, until dough is doubled, at least one hour.

Filling: Combine sugar and cocoa in a small bowl; set aside.
Continued on next page

Chocolate Babka/Continued:

Punch out the dough on a well-floured surface and leave it to rest for 5 minutes. Gently stretch and pull the dough with floured hands into a 10-inch x 16-inch rectangle.

Brush the rectangle with 2 Tbl. melted margarine. Sprinkle the sugar/chocolate mixture over the margarine and then sprinkle the chocolate chips over the top.

Roll up the dough lengthwise, gently stretching the dough and then pinching the seam shut with your fingers. Transfer babka to a greased cookie sheet, seam side down. Let rise again in a warm place for about 1 hour.

Preheat oven to 350 degrees.

Bake babka for 20 minutes. Brush the top with olive oil.

Bake an additional 10 to 20 minutes, until it is lightly browned and feels hollow when gently knocked with your knuckles.

Cool thoroughly before serving.

**This is a time intensive dessert, but fairly easy if you spread it out over the course of your day. I prepare the dough in the morning and let it rise for a couple of hours. Then I prepare the filling and create the babka, placing it on the greased baking sheet to rise again. I then bake it right before dinner so it has time to cool. Treat your family; this dessert is well worth the effort!

Streusel Raspberry Dessert Bread

Sweet and awesome, this is not your grandma's "fuddy-duddy" dessert bread. This delicious treat tastes so good and rich; they'll never know it is dairy and egg free.

1¾ C flour, divided
½ C sugar
2 tsp. baking powder
½ C plus 2 Tbl. dairy-free margarine, divided
1½ Tbl. water, 1½ Tbl. oil, 1 tsp. baking powder; mixed together
½ C water
½ C raspberry preserves
¼ C brown sugar, firmly packed

Preheat oven to 375 degrees. Grease loaf pan.

In a large bowl, whisk together 1½ C flour, sugar, and baking powder. Set aside.

In a small glass bowl, melt ½ C margarine. Add water/oil/baking powder mixture and water, stirring well.

Add wet ingredients to the dry ingredients, stirring until just moistened. Fold in raspberry preserves.

Pour into prepared pan. Set aside.

Combine remaining ¼ C flour, 2 Tbl. margarine, and brown sugar with a fork. Sprinkle evenly over batter.

Bake 55 minutes or until a tester comes out clean.

Scones with Streusel Topping

Okay--if you are on any kind of diet or carbohydrate avoidance, DO NOT make these scones. They are SO tasty you and your family will not be able to stay away from them! These make a great impression on company.   The savory scone is topped with a scrumptious streusel.

2 C flour
¼ C sugar
2 tsp. baking powder
¼ tsp. baking soda
¼ tsp. salt
¼ C dairy-free margarine, chilled and cut into pieces
¾ C water
Scone topping (recipe below)

Preheat oven to 450 degrees. Grease a baking sheet.

Whisk together flour, sugar, baking powder, baking soda, and salt. Cut in margarine with a pastry blender until crumbly.

Add water and combine. Knead a couple of times in the bowl. Place dough on prepared baking sheet and pat into 8-inch circle. Set aside.

Scone Topping:
1 Tbl. dairy-free margarine, melted
¼ C oats
¼ C brown sugar, firmly packed
1 Tbl. flour

Melt margarine in a small, glass bowl. Stir in the oats, brown sugar, and flour with a fork.

Pat mixture onto the top surface of the prepared dough with your hands. Cut dough into 12 wedges, but do not separate the wedges.

Bake 15 minutes, or until lightly browned. Serve warm.

Blueberry Muffins

I never knew blueberry muffins could taste so good! The topping on these really sets them apart, making them taste bakery-fresh! I use the topping on other things (such as zucchini bread) as well.

2 C flour
2 tsp. baking powder
½ tsp. salt
½ C dairy-free margarine
1 C plus 2 Tbl. sugar
3 Tbl. water, 3 Tbl. oil, 2 tsp. baking powder; mixed together
1 tsp. vanilla
½ C water
2½ C blueberries (fresh or frozen)
topping: 1 Tbl. sugar mixed with ¼ tsp. ground nutmeg

Preheat oven to 375 degrees. Line muffin tin with paper liners.

Whisk together flour, baking powder, and salt. Set aside.

In a large, glass bowl melt the margarine. Beat in the sugar until fluffy. Add water/oil/baking powder mixture, vanilla, and water; combine.

Add dry ingredients to wet ingredients and stir thoroughly.

Fold in blueberries.

Scoop batter into muffin cups. Sprinkle the tops with the nutmeg-sugar mixture.

Bake 25 to 30 minutes or until tester comes out clean.

Let muffins cool completely before serving.

Apple Muffins with Streusel Topping

My husband loves these muffins. He says they taste just like store-bought muffins.

1½ C flour
½ C sugar
2 tsp. baking powder
1 tsp. cinnamon
¼ tsp. ground allspice
¼ tsp. baking soda
¼ tsp. salt
¼ C dairy-free margarine, melted
1 C water
3 Tbl. water, 3 Tbl. oil, 2 tsp. baking powder; mixed together
1 C apple, diced with intact peel
Streusel Topping (see below)

Preheat oven to 375 degrees. Line muffin tin with liners.

Whisk together flour, sugar, baking powder, cinnamon, allspice, baking soda, and salt in a large bowl. Set aside.

In a separate glass bowl, melt the margarine and then beat in the water and the water/oil/baking powder mixture until well blended. Stir in diced apple.

Add wet ingredients to the dry ingredients and stir until moistened. Pour the batter into muffin liners. Top with the Streusel Topping.

Streusel Topping:
4 Tbl. dairy-free margarine, melted
½ C flour
6 Tbl. sugar
½ tsp. cinnamon

Mix streusel-topping ingredients with a fork until the mixture is crumbly. Top each muffin with a heaping tablespoon of streusel.

Bake muffins 20 to 25 minutes, or until tester comes out clean. Let cool completely before serving (IF you can wait!).

S'more Muffins

If S'mores are your favorite camping treat, you'll love these muffins. Little chunky surprises are found throughout these rich tasting muffins.

1½ C flour
½ C dairy-free, egg-free, nut-free graham cracker coarse crumbs (about 7 squares)
¼ C packed brown sugar
1 tsp. baking soda
½ tsp. salt
½ C dairy-free margarine
1½ Tbl. water, 1½ Tbl. oil, 1 tsp. baking powder; mixed together
1¼ C soymilk—plain or vanilla
1/8 C vegetable oil
1 C dairy-free, nut free chocolate chips
1¼ C egg-free miniature marshmallows, divided

Preheat oven to 375 degrees. Line a muffin tin with paper liners.

In a large bowl, whisk together flour, graham cracker crumbs, brown sugar, soda, and salt. Set aside.

Melt the margarine in a separate glass bowl. Stir in the water/oil/baking powder mixture, soymilk, and oil.

Stir wet ingredients into the dry ingredients just until moistened. Fold in chocolate chips and 1 C marshmallows.

Fill muffin cups 3/4 full. Sprinkle with remaining marshmallows.

Bake for 15 minutes, or until tester comes out clean.

Jelly-Filled Muffins

My kids love to find the "hidden" surprise in these.

2 C flour
2 tsp. baking powder
¼ tsp. salt
½ C dairy-free shortening
1 C sugar
1 tsp. vanilla
2/3 C soymilk--plain or vanilla
3 Tbl. water, 3 Tbl. oil, 2 tsp. baking powder, mixed together
about 4 Tbl. jelly—your favorite flavor

Preheat oven to 375 degrees. Line a muffin tin with paper
liners.

Whisk together flour, baking powder, and salt. Set aside.

In a large bowl, beat the shortening and sugar until fluffy.
Stir in vanilla, soymilk, and water/oil/baking powder mixture.

Add dry ingredients to the wet ingredients and stir until
moistened.

Spoon the batter into the muffin cups until half full. Drop
about 1 tsp. of your favorite jelly into the center of the dough.

Top with the remaining batter, spreading with two spoons to
cover all of the jelly.

Bake 25 minutes, or until tester comes out clean.

Pumpkin Muffins

These wonderfully moist muffins are perfect on a cool autumn day.

1¾ C flour
1/3 C sugar
2 tsp. baking powder
1 tsp. cinnamon
½ tsp. nutmeg
1/8 tsp. ground cloves
½ C canned pumpkin
1½ Tbl. water, 1½ Tbl. oil, 1 tsp. baking powder; mixed together
¾ C soymilk--plain or vanilla
¼ C vegetable oil
Streusel Topping (see following), optional

Preheat oven to 400 degrees. Grease muffin tin with dairy-free cooking spray. Do not use paper liners.

In a large bowl whisk together flour, sugar, baking powder, and spices. Set aside.

In a separate bowl combine pumpkin, water/oil/baking powder mixture, soymilk, and oil.

Add wet ingredients to dry ingredients and stir until moistened.

Fill muffin compartments about two-thirds full. Sprinkle Streusel topping over the batter (if using).

Bake 20 minutes, or until tester comes out clean.

Streusel Topping:
4 Tbl. dairy-free margarine, melted
½ C flour
6 Tbl. sugar
½ tsp. cinnamon

Mix streusel-topping ingredients until the mixture is the size of peas.

Chocolate Pretzels

My boys love these fun treats. We have had pretzel parties, where kids twisted and decorated the pretzels with colored sugar.

2½ C flour
½ C unsweetened cocoa powder
½ tsp. baking soda
¼ tsp. salt
2/3 C dairy-free margarine
1 C sugar
2 tsp. vanilla
3 Tbl. water, 3 Tbl. oil, 2 tsp. baking powder; mixed together
confectioners' sugar or colored sugar

Preheat oven to 350 degrees.

Whisk together flour, cocoa powder, baking soda and salt. Set aside.

In a large, glass bowl melt the margarine. Beat in sugar and vanilla until thoroughly combined. Add water/oil/ baking powder mixture and stir well.

Add dry ingredients to the wet ingredients and blend thoroughly.

Divide dough into 24 pieces. Roll each piece into a 12-inch long strip (fun part for kids!). Shape and twist strips into pretzel shapes (or any pleasing shape) on cookie sheet.

Bake 8 minutes or until set. Cool slightly before moving to wire rack. Sprinkle with confectioners' sugar or colored sugar.

Sweet Pretzels

These pretzels are a great project, fun and yummy.

3 C flour
1 tsp. baking powder
½ tsp. baking soda
½ tsp. salt
½ C dairy-free margarine
1 C sugar
1½ Tbl. water, 1½ Tbl. oil, 1 tsp. baking powder; mixed together
1 tsp. vanilla
2/3 C water
colored sugar

Whisk flour, baking powder, baking soda, and salt together. Set aside.

In a large, glass bowl melt the margarine. Beat in the sugar until fluffy. Add water/oil/baking powder mixture and vanilla; beat well. Stir in the remaining water.

Add dry ingredients to the wet ingredients and beat until well mixed.

Cover with plastic wrap and chill overnight.

Preheat oven to 425 degrees.

Divide dough in half. On a floured surface, roll each half into a 10-inch x 5-inch rectangle. Cut into 5-inch x ½-inch strips. Roll each strip into a rope. Shape each rope into a pretzel (or any fun shape).

Place pretzels on an ungreased cookie sheet. Brush with water. Sprinkle with sugar.

Bake 5 to 6 minutes or until lightly browned. Cool on a wire rack.

Biscuits

These biscuits are a must on our dinner table most nights. They are so quick and delicious; you'll add them to your repertoire.

1 C flour
1 C whole-wheat flour
1 Tbl. baking powder
2 tsp. sugar
½ tsp. cream of tartar
¼ tsp. salt
½ C dairy-free shortening
1 C plain-flavored soymilk

Preheat oven to 450 degrees.

In a large bowl whisk together flour, baking powder, sugar, cream of tartar, and salt.

Cut in shortening with a pastry blender until mixture resembles coarse crumbs. Add soymilk all at once. Stir until dough is formed.

Drop dough by tablespoons, making nine biscuits.

Bake 10 to 12 minutes, or until golden brown.

**Combine three tablespoons of dough on the baking sheet if making five large biscuits (for Tarragon Chicken Bun Boats).

Sweet Potato Biscuits

These biscuits are a great addition to a holiday table such as Thanksgiving. They are moist, dense, and sweet.

3 C flour
1/3 C yellow corn meal
2½ tsp. baking powder
½ tsp. salt
1/3 C dairy-free margarine, chilled
1 C sweet potato, cooked and mashed
½ C water
2 Tbl. honey

Preheat oven to 400 degrees.

Whisk together flour, corn meal, baking powder, and salt. Cut in margarine with a pastry blender until mixture resembles coarse crumbs.

Add mashed sweet potato, water, and honey; stir just until moist.

Turn dough out onto a floured surface; knead dough a few times. Form dough into a 9-inch square with your hands. Cut into 16 squares.

Place squares onto baking sheet with some room between each biscuit.

Bake 20 minutes or until golden.

Sweet Corn Bread

This is the perfect compliment to Split Pea soup or Chili. The texture is great.

1½ C flour
2/3 C sugar
½ C corn meal
1 Tbl. baking powder
½ tsp. salt
3 Tbl. dairy-free margarine
1¼ C plain-flavored soymilk
1½ Tbl. water, 1½ Tbl. oil, 1 tsp. baking powder; mixed together
1/3 C oil

Preheat oven to 350 degrees. Grease an 8-inch square baking pan.

Whisk together flour, sugar, corn meal, baking powder, and salt in a large bowl. Set aside.

Melt margarine in large glass bowl. Add soymilk, water/oil/baking powder mixture, and oil; mix well.

Add dry ingredients to wet ingredients; stir just until blended. Pour into prepared pan.

Bake for 35 minutes, or until tester comes out clean.

Banana Bread

This version of the home-cooked favorite is just the right texture: dense, moist, and filling. The orange adds a nice zip.

1¼ C flour
½ C "safe" whole-wheat flour
¼ C "safe" wheat germ
1 C sugar
¼ tsp. salt
2 tsp. baking soda
4 mashed ripe bananas
½ C vegetable oil
2 Tbl. orange juice
3/4 tsp. grated orange peel
optional additions: dairy-free, nut-free chocolate chips, egg-free mini-marshmallows

Preheat oven to 350 degrees. Grease a loaf pan.

Whisk together flour, whole-wheat flour, wheat germ, sugar, baking soda, and salt. Set aside.

In a large bowl, combine mashed bananas, oil, orange juice, and orange peel.

Add dry ingredients to wet ingredients and stir till blended.

Pour batter into prepared pan.

Bake 50 to 55 minutes, or until tester comes out clean.

Remove from oven and cool for at least 15 minutes on a wire rack.

Zucchini Bread

This moist, sweet bread has a great texture and is rich and tasty.

3 C flour
½ tsp. baking powder
1 tsp. salt
2 tsp. cinnamon
1 tsp. baking soda
2 C grated zucchini
4½ Tbl. water, 4½ Tbl. oil, 1 Tbl. baking powder; mixed together
1 C vegetable oil
1 Tbl. vanilla
2 C sugar
Topping: 2 Tbl. sugar mixed with ½ tsp. ground nutmeg

Preheat oven to 350 degrees. Grease and flour two 9-inch x 5-inch loaf pans.

Whisk together flour, baking powder, salt, cinnamon, and baking soda. Set aside.

Combine grated zucchini, water/oil/baking powder mixture, oil, vanilla, and sugar in a separate bowl.

Add wet ingredients to the dry ingredients and mix well.

Pour batter into the two loaf pans. Sprinkle the sugar/nutmeg topping evenly over both loaves.

Bake for 1 hour, or until tester inserted near center of loaves comes out clean.

Focaccia Bread

This tasty bread, popular in restaurants, is very easy to make and a welcome addition to the dinner table.

1 C warm water
1½ tsp. active dry yeast
1 tsp. sugar
1 tsp. salt
1 to 2 Tbl. freshly snipped rosemary
3½ C flour
dairy-free, egg-free cooking spray
1 to 2 Tbl. olive oil

Sprinkle yeast over the water in a large bowl. Let sit for 10 minutes. Stir in sugar, salt and rosemary.

Add flour, one cup at a time, with a wooden spoon. After all of the flour is incorporated, knead dough for a few minutes until smooth.

Spray cooking spray on bowl and the top of the dough. Cover and let rise in a warm place until doubled in size.

Punch down the dough and transfer to a floured surface. Knead dough for another 5 to 8 minutes, until elastic and smooth.

Preheat oven to 400 degrees.

Roll dough out into a 10-inch diameter circle. Let the dough circle rest for about 10 minutes.

Place the bread dough onto a greased baking sheet and brush olive oil over the top.

Bake for about 25 minutes, or until lightly browned.

Marvelous Monkey Bread

This rich dessert bread will satisfy the sweet tooth of everyone in your family. The roll portions are deliciously covered in a sweet, gooey topping that no one can resist.

24 frozen, dairy-free, egg-free, nut-free dinner rolls
¼ C dairy-free, egg-free, nut-free vanilla pudding mix (half of a small box)
1 C brown sugar
2 Tbl. cinnamon
½ C dairy-free margarine, melted

Liberally coat a Bundt pan with dairy-free margarine. Arrange frozen rolls equally around pan.

Combine pudding mix, brown sugar, and cinnamon in a small bowl. Sprinkle sugar mixture equally over the rolls.

Pour melted margarine evenly over sugared rolls.

Place a towel over the pan and let sit over night.

Preheat oven to 375 degrees.

Bake for 20 to 25 minutes, until tester comes out clean.

Let the bread sit in the pan for 5 minutes, then invert onto a plate.

DAIRY-FREE, EGG-FREE, NUT-FREE DESSERTS

Here are our favorite desserts that will pass muster with the whole family. All of the following treats passed my "good texture" requirements. Happy baking!

COOKIES

Oatmeal Cranberry Cookies

The boy's love these cookies and family members request them. They so good with the sweet and tangy mix of cranberries and oatmeal.

2 C oats
2 C flour
1 tsp. baking soda
1 tsp. ground cinnamon
1 tsp. salt
1 C dairy-free margarine
1¼ C brown sugar, firmly packed
½ C sugar
3 Tbl. water, 3 Tbl. oil, 2 tsp. baking powder; mixed together
2 tsp. vanilla
2 Tbl. water
1½ C dried, sweetened cranberries

Preheat oven to 350 degrees. Grease cookie sheets.

Whisk together oats, flour, baking soda, cinnamon, and salt. Set aside.

In a large, glass bowl melt the margarine. Add sugars and beat until fluffy. Mix in water/oil/baking powder mixture, vanilla, and water.

Add dry ingredients to wet ingredients and stir until combined. Fold in cranberries. Drop by the teaspoonfuls onto prepared cookie sheets.

Bake 12 minutes, or until golden brown. Cool on wire rack.

Glazed Raspberry Crunch Cookies

I always bring these tasty cookies to gatherings. The tangy lemon glaze adds a delightful zip to the sweet raspberry cookie.

1 C flour
2 Tbl. cornstarch
¼ tsp. baking powder
¼ tsp. salt
5 Tbl. dairy-free margarine
1/3 C sugar
1¾ tsp. vanilla, divided
1½ Tbl. water, 1½ Tbl. oil, 1 tsp. baking powder; mixed together
½ C raspberry preserves
½ C confectioners' sugar
2 tsp. lemon juice (fresh is best)

Preheat oven to 375 degrees. Grease a cookie sheet.

Whisk together flour, cornstarch, baking powder, and salt in a medium bowl. Set aside.

In large glass bowl melt the margarine; beat in sugar until well blended. Add 1½ tsp. vanilla and water/oil/baking powder mixture and combine.

Add dry ingredients to wet ingredients. Mix until thoroughly blended.

Divide dough in half. On a floured surface, roll each half into a 12-inch log. Place logs on prepared cookie sheet. Carve a ½ -inch groove down the length of each log. Spoon preserves into this furrow.

Bake 15 minutes, or until light brown in color. Transfer to cutting board. Set aside.

In a small bowl, combine confectioners' sugar, lemon juice, and ¼ tsp. vanilla. Drizzle over warm logs. Cut each log diagonally into 12 slices.

Chocolate Chip Cookies, Kingma Style

These cookies won 'hands down' in my personal dairy-free, egg-free, chocolate-chip cookie taste contest. They are light and tasty, sweet and satisfying.

1¼ C flour
½ tsp. baking soda
½ C dairy-free margarine
½ C sugar
1 tsp. vanilla
1 Tbl. water, 1 Tbl. Balsamic vinegar, and 1 tsp. baking powder; mixed together
1 C dairy-free, nut-free chocolate chips
1 C optional additions: coconut, oatmeal, Crispy Rice cereal, raisins, mini marshmallows

Preheat oven to 375 degrees.

Whisk together flour and baking soda in a medium sized bowl. Set aside.

Melt the margarine in a large, glass bowl. Add sugar and beat until fluffy. Add vanilla and water/vinegar/baking powder mixture. Combine.

Add dry ingredients to the wet ingredients and blend well.

Fold in chocolate chips and any optional additions.

Drop, by the teaspoonful, onto ungreased cookie sheets and bake for 11 to 13 minutes, until golden brown.

Button Cookies

These cute, little cookies are often requested at our house. They are colorful, sweet, and pop-in-your-mouth tasty.

1½ C flour
¼ C cornstarch
¼ tsp. salt
5 Tbl. dairy-free margarine
¾ C confectioners' sugar
2 Tbl. vegetable oil
4 Tbl. water
1½ tsp. vanilla
2 colors of food coloring
½ C confectioners' sugar

Preheat oven to 350 degrees.

Whisk together flour, cornstarch, and salt. Set aside.

In a large, glass bowl melt the margarine. Add confectioners' sugar, oil, water, and vanilla. Beat until fluffy.

Add dry ingredients to the wet ingredients and mix just until blended.

Split dough in half. Add desired amount of food coloring to each half, blending well.

Roll dough into ¾ inch balls and place on ungreased cookie sheets.

Bake 10 minutes, or until lightly browned.

While cookies are baking, sift ½ C confectioners' sugar into a shallow dish. When cookies are finished baking, remove from oven and roll immediately in sugar. Cool on wire racks.

Elephant Ears

These cookies are great to make with your kids. They
especially enjoy the patting part. And they are sweetie-
delicious.

4 Tbl. dairy-free margarine (divided)
1 C flour
2 Tbl. sugar
½ tsp. baking powder
½ tsp. salt
1/3 C plain or vanilla soymilk
mixture: 3 Tbl. sugar combined with 1 tsp. cinnamon sugar

Preheat oven to 425 degrees. Grease cookie sheet.

In a large, glass bowl melt 3 Tbl. margarine. Add flour, sugar,
baking powder, and salt, blending thoroughly. Stir in soymilk
to form dough.

Sprinkle a surface lightly with flour; turn dough onto surface.
Knead 10 times. Pat dough into a 9-inch by 5-inch rectangle.

Melt the remaining 1 Tbl. margarine. Brush melted margarine
evenly over the dough. Sprinkle with the sugar cinnamon
mixture.

Roll dough up, beginning at narrow end. Pinch edge of dough
into roll to seal. Cut into four equal pieces with knife.

Place sections, cut sides up, on cookie sheet.

Pat each piece into a 6-inch circle. Sprinkle with additional
sugar.

Bake 8 to 10 minutes, or until golden brown. Immediately
remove from cookie sheet. Let cool on wire rack.

Cranberry Cookies with Coconut

These sweet cookies, infused with the blend of orange, coconut, and cranberry, are a hit at Christmas time!

3¼ C flour
1 tsp. baking powder
¼ tsp. salt
1½ C dairy-free margarine
2 C sugar
1 Tbl. grated orange peel
2 tsp. vanilla
1½ C dried cranberries
1½ C sweetened flaked coconut

Preheat oven to 350 degrees. Grease cookie sheets.

Whisk together flour, baking powder, and salt. Set aside.

In a large, glass bowl melt the margarine. Add sugar, orange peel, and vanilla. Beat well until fluffy.

Add dry ingredients to the wet ingredients. Mix until thoroughly combined.

Fold in cranberries and coconut.

Shape dough into 1-inch balls and place about 2 inches apart on prepared cookie sheets.

Bake 8 to 11 minutes, just until cookie edges begin to brown.

Let cookies cool on sheets for 5 minutes and then transfer to racks to cool completely.

Be My Honey Cookies

Honey sweet for the honeys in your life!

1½ C flour
½ tsp. baking soda
½ tsp. salt
½ tsp. cinnamon
½ C dairy-free margarine
½ C packed brown sugar
½ C honey
1½ Tbl. water, 1½ Tbl. oil, 1 tsp. baking powder; mixed together

Preheat oven to 375 degrees.

Whisk together flour, baking soda, salt, and cinnamon. Set aside.

In a large, glass bowl melt the margarine. Beat in brown sugar, honey, and water/oil/baking powder mixture until smooth.

Add dry ingredients to the wet ingredients. Stir to combine.

Drop dough by teaspoonfuls onto ungreased cookie sheets.

Bake until light brown around the edges, 7 to 9 minutes.

Let stand 3 to 5 minutes on the cookie sheet and then remove to cool completely on wire racks.

Orangey Coconut Cookies

These cookies taste so decadent with the orange zest flavor. They are chewy with a terrific texture and are absolutely scrumptious!

1 C flour
1 C oats
1 C firmly packed brown sugar
1 tsp. baking soda
1 tsp. baking powder
½ C dairy-free shortening
1½ Tbl. grated orange peel
1/3 C orange juice
¼ C flaked sweetened coconut

Preheat oven to 350 degrees. Grease cookie sheets.

In a large bowl, whisk together flour, oats, brown sugar, baking soda, and baking powder.

Cut in shortening with a pastry blender until crumbly. Add orange peel and orange juice; stir until completely combined.

Fold in coconut.

Drop dough by teaspoonfuls 2 inches apart onto prepared cookie sheets.

Bake for 10 minutes, remove from cookie sheets, and cool completely.

Gingerbread People

These cookies are naturally dairy- and egg- free and so fun to make! We have enjoyed a couple "Gingerbread People Decorating" Parties.

2½ C flour
¾ tsp. salt
¾ tsp. ground ginger
½ tsp. baking soda
¼ tsp. ground allspice
½ C dairy-free shortening
½ C sugar
½ C dark molasses
¼ C water
Toppings: raisins
             frosting
             "safe" candy

Whisk together flour, salt, ginger, baking soda, and allspice. Set aside.

In a large bowl, blend shortening, sugar, molasses, and water until thoroughly combined.

Add dry ingredients to shortening mixture and stir until well blended.

Cover and refrigerate until chilled, about 2 hours (or overnight).

Preheat oven to 375 degrees.

Roll out dough on lightly floured surface to ¼ inch thickness. Cut with people-shaped cookie cutters. Lift carefully with spatula. Place on ungreased cookie sheets.

Bake until set, about 8 to 10 minutes. Cool.

Decorate with frosting, raisins, or safe candy.

Snickerdoodles

These crunchy, sweet cookies are a hit at my house.

2 ¾ C flour
2 tsp. Cream of Tartar
1 tsp. soda
¼ tsp. salt
½ C dairy-free margarine
½ C vegetable shortening
1 ½ C sugar
3 Tbl. water, 3 Tbl. oil, 2 tsp. baking powder; mixed together
Topping: 2 Tbl. sugar mixed with 2 tsp. cinnamon

Preheat oven to 400 degrees. Grease cookie sheets.

Whisk together the flour, Cream of Tartar, soda, and salt. Set aside.

In a large, glass mixing bowl melt the margarine. Add the shortening and stir well until the shortening is incorporated. Add sugar and water/oil/baking powder mixture and cream well.

Add dry ingredients to wet ingredients and stir to combine.

Drop dough by tablespoons on prepared cookie sheets.

With the prongs of a fork dipped in flour, flatten out the dough.

Sprinkle cinnamon sugar topping on top.

Bake 8 to 10 minutes, or until golden brown.

Candy Cane Cookies

These cookies are a Christmas favorite and are fun to make.

½ C dairy-free margarine
½ C vegetable shortening
1 C confectioners' sugar
1½ Tbl. water, 1½ Tbl. oil, 1 tsp. baking powder; mixed together
1¼ tsp. peppermint extract
1 tsp. vanilla
2½ C flour
1 tsp. salt
½ tsp. red food color
optional topping: ½ C crushed dairy-free, nut-free candy cane mixed with ½ C sugar

Preheat oven to 375 degrees.

In a large glass bowl, melt the margarine and shortening together. Add confectioners' sugar, water/oil/baking powder mixture, peppermint extract, and vanilla; mix well.

Blend in flour and salt.

Divide dough in half; add red food coloring to half and incorporate well.

Create 4-inch ropes out of one-teaspoon dough balls. Place a red rope next to a white rope; press together lightly and twist. Curve the tops down to form a candy cane shape.

Bake cookies for 9 minutes, until very light brown.

Mix candy crumbles and sugar and sprinkle over the top of the cookies (optional).

Sugar Cookies

Every mother needs a delicious sugar cookie recipe to share with her children. Cookie cutters are available for every occasion and every child loves to decorate them. Round up that rolling pin, it is baking time!

2 C flour
¼ tsp. salt
12 Tbl. dairy-free margarine
¾ C sugar
1½ Tbl. water, 1½ Tbl. oil, 1 tsp. baking powder; mixed together
1 tsp. vanilla
colored sugars or toppings of your choice

Whisk together the flour and salt; set aside.

Melt the margarine in a large, glass bowl. Add sugar and beat until fluffy. Add water/oil/baking powder mixture and vanilla and mix well.

Add the dry ingredients to the wet ingredients and blend just until combined.

Form the dough into a ball, cover with plastic wrap and chill in the refrigerator for at least an hour.

Preheat oven to 325 degrees.

Roll out dough on a floured surface to a 1/3-inch thickness. These tend to be a bit crumbly, so they need to be a bit thick. Cut dough with cookie cutters and carefully transfer to an ungreased cookie sheet. Decorate with sugars or toppings.

Bake for 13 to 15 minutes, until very lightly brown.

These cookies are a bit hard to handle (eggs make dough easier to work), but manageable.

Santa's Whiskers Cookies

These zippy cookies are one of our holiday favorites!

¾ C dairy-free margarine
2 C flour
¾ C sugar
1 Tbl. soymilk: vanilla or plain
1 tsp. vanilla
¾ C finely chopped maraschino cherries
1/3 C Crispy Rice cereal or crushed Corn Flake-type cereal
¾ C coconut

Melt margarine in a large, glass bowl. Add 1-cup flour, sugar, soymilk, and vanilla and thoroughly blend. Stir in remaining 1-cup flour. Fold in cherries and cereal.

Shape into two 8-inch logs. Roll in the coconut, pressing coconut into the mixture.

Wrap in waxed paper and chill for at least 2 hours.

Preheat oven to 375 degrees.

Cut ¼-inch slices off the log. Place on ungreased cookie sheet.

Bake for 10 minutes, or until slightly brown around the edges.

Chocolate Sandwich Cookies

These cookies are a fun addition to your baking repertoire!

2 (1-ounce) squares dairy-free, nut-free, unsweetened chocolate
½ C dairy-free margarine
1 C brown sugar
1½ Tbl. water, 1½ Tbl. oil, 1 tsp. baking powder; mixed together
1 tsp. vanilla
1/8 tsp. baking soda
2 C flour
Filling (recipe follows)

Melt chocolate in a small saucepan on the stove, constantly stirring. Set aside.

Melt margarine in a large, glass bowl. Add brown sugar and mix well.

Stir in water/oil/baking powder mixture, vanilla, baking soda, and melted chocolate. Beat until fluffy. Add flour and stir until dough is formed.

Divide dough into four sections. Roll each section into a 1½-inch diameter log. Wrap and chill for at least an hour.

Preheat oven to 375 degrees. Cut logs into 1/8-inch slices.

Bake 6 to 7 minutes on ungreased cookie sheets. Assemble cookies after they have completely cooled.

Filling:
2 Tbl. dairy-free margarine
1½ C confectioners' sugar
3 to 4 Tbl. soymilk: plain or vanilla
flavoring: ¼ tsp. peppermint or ½ tsp. vanilla
green food coloring (if making mint flavored cookies)

Melt margarine in a medium, glass bowl. Add sugar and soymilk and cream together. Stir in flavoring and food coloring (if using) until incorporated. Frost one cookie and place another cookie on top, making a cookie sandwich.

Eli's Chocolate Marshmallow Cookies

These tasty cookies remind me of a brownie and are irresistible.

1¾ C flour
½ C unsweetened cocoa powder
½ tsp. salt
1 tsp. baking soda
1 C shortening
½ C brown sugar
½ C sugar
¼ C soymilk: plain or vanilla
1 tsp. vanilla
large egg-free marshmallows, cut in half

Preheat oven to 350 degrees.

Whisk flour, cocoa powder, salt, and baking soda together in a medium bowl. Set aside.

In a large bowl, cream shortening, brown sugar, sugar, soymilk, and vanilla together until well combined.

Add the flour mixture to the shortening mixture and mix well.

Drop dough by the tablespoon on ungreased cookie sheets. Bake 8 minutes.

Remove trays from the oven and place half of a marshmallow in the center of each cookie. Return cookies to the oven and bake an additional 2 minutes. Let cool completely.

Optional: top with chocolate frosting.

Chocolate Frosting:
½ C dairy-free margarine
2/3 confectioners' sugar
¼ C water,
1 tsp. vanilla
½ C unsweetened cocoa powder

Cream all ingredients together in a bowl. Frost cooled cookies.

Grandma's No Bake Cookies

My boys love these "Blast from the Past" cookies that my grandma would make me when I was little.

3¼ C oats
½ C shredded coconut
½ C cocoa powder
¾ C dairy-free margarine
¼ C soy milk: plain or vanilla
2 C sugar
½ tsp. vanilla

Whisk together the oatmeal, coconut, and cocoa powder in a large bowl. Set aside.

In a saucepan, combine margarine, soy milk, and sugar.

Cook over medium heat, stirring constantly until mixture reaches a boil. Boil for one minute. Remove from heat and stir in vanilla (watch for splatters!).

Pour warm, wet ingredients into dry ingredients and mix well.

Drop by tablespoons onto wax paper and let cool and harden. Enjoy!

CAKES

Easy Chocolate Cake

I cannot rave enough about this cake. It turns out perfect every time and tastes so rich and delicious that you'll never use another chocolate cake recipe ever again. Simply the best!

1½ C flour
1/3 C unsweetened cocoa powder
1 tsp. baking soda
½ tsp. salt
1 C sugar
½ C vegetable oil
1 C cold water
2 tsp. vanilla
2 Tbl. white vinegar

Preheat oven to 375 degrees. Grease and flour a 9-inch x 13-inch cake pan.

Whisk together flour, cocoa powder, baking soda, salt, and sugar. Set aside.

Combine oil, water, and vanilla in a large bowl.

Add dry ingredients to the wet ingredients. Stir to combine.

Add vinegar and quickly stir until combined.

Bake 25 to 30 minutes or until tester inserted in the center comes out clean.

Special Snack Cake

This is a deluxe, special-treat cake that sends my family and I into chocolate rapture. It tastes just like the Ho Ho snack cakes.

Cake Batter:
3 C flour
2 C sugar
2 tsp. baking soda
2/3 C unsweetened cocoa powder
2 C, plus 2 tsp. water
2/3 C vegetable oil
2 tsp. vanilla
2 tsp. white vinegar

Preheat oven to 350 degrees. Grease a 9-inch x 13-inch pan.

Whisk together flour, sugar, baking soda, and coca powder. Set aside.

Combine water, oil, vanilla and vinegar in a separate, large bowl.

Add dry ingredients to wet ingredients; stir to combine.

Pour into prepared pan.

Bake for 35 minutes, or until tester comes out clean. Cool.

Put in refrigerator for 30 minutes before putting on the first topping.

First Topping:
1¼ C dairy-free, nut-free, nondairy creamer (Be sure to check with manufacturer to ensure creamer is indeed dairy-free and not made on equipment with any nut creamers.)
5 Tbl. flour
½ C dairy-free margarine
1 C dairy-free shortening
1 C confectioners' sugar

In a small saucepan, whisk together nondairy creamer and flour. Cook over medium heat until thickened. Cool.

In a large, glass bowl melt the margarine. Blend in the shortening until melted and combined. Stir in the confectioners' sugar.

Add cooled creamer mixture to the margarine mixture. With an electric mixer (important!), beat on high 5 minutes. Spread on cooled cake. Place cake back in the refrigerator.

Second Topping:
½ C dairy-free margarine
3 squares dairy-free, nut-free semi-sweet chocolate baking squares
1½ C confectioners' sugar
1½ Tbl. water, 1½ Tbl. oil, 1 tsp. baking powder; mixed together
1 tsp. vanilla
1 tsp. water

In a saucepan over medium heat, melt together the margarine and semi-sweet chocolate, stirring constantly. Set aside to cool.

Combine confectioners' sugar, water/oil/baking powder mixture, vanilla, and water in a medium bowl.

Stir in cooled chocolate mixture and thoroughly combine.

Spread this chocolate mixture evenly over the first topping.

Store in refrigerator until ready to serve.

Streusel-Layered Coffeecake

This is my best-known and loved treat in my extended family.
I bring it to share at any type of gathering.

Streusel:
6 Tbl. dairy-free margarine, melted
1½ C brown sugar
6 Tbl. flour
3 tsp. cinnamon

Batter:
3 C flour
5 tsp. baking powder
1 tsp. salt
11 Tbl. dairy-free margarine, melted
1½ Tbl. water, 1½ Tbl. oil, 1 tsp. baking powder; mixed together
1½ C sugar
1 C plain or vanilla soymilk
2 tsp. vanilla

Preheat oven to 375 degrees. Grease 9-inch x 13-inch pan.

Combine streusel mixture with a fork; set aside.

Whisk together flour, baking powder, and salt. Set aside.

In large glass bowl melt the margarine. Add water/oil/baking powder mixture and sugar and beat until well combined. Stir in soymilk and vanilla.

Add dry ingredients to wet ingredients and stir until moistened.

Pour half of batter into pan. Sprinkle evenly with half of the streusel mixture. Repeat.

Bake 25 to 30 minutes, or until tester comes out clean.

Rhubarb Cake

This is actually one of my all-time favorite cakes and my kids love it as well. It is sweet and a touch tangy, but is tempered by the cake on top. Delicious!

3 to 4 C skinned, chopped rhubarb
1 small package of red Jell-O (strawberry!)
1 C sugar
½ a large bag of large-sized marshmallows
"safe" white cake (see following)

Preheat oven to 375 degrees.

Toss the rhubarb with the Jell-O powder and spread into a single layer on the bottom of an 8-inch x 11-inch baking pan. Sprinkle the sugar evenly across the top. Evenly spread a layer of marshmallows over the sugared rhubarb mixture. Spread the cake mixture (see below) evenly over the top.

Bake 30 minutes, or until tester inserted in the center comes out clean. I suggest putting a cookie sheet under the baking pan for spills.

White Cake:

1/3 C shortening
¾ C sugar
½ tsp. salt
3 Tbl. plus ¼ tsp. flour
3 Tbl. water
2¼ tsp. vegetable oil

2 tsp. lemon juice (fresh is best)
1½ C plus 2 Tbl. flour
¾ C water
3½ tsp. baking powder

In a large bowl, cream shortening, sugar, and salt together. Set aside.

In a small bowl, combine 3 Tbl. plus ¼ tsp. flour, 3 Tbl. water, and 2¼ tsp. oil; stir well. Combine with the shortening mixture. Beat well. Stir in lemon juice.

Add remaining flour and water, stirring until moist. Add baking powder; beat well and quickly.

Spread mixture with a spatula over prepared rhubarb mixture in pan. Bake as directed above.

Lemon Pound Cake

You cannot tell this delicious cake is made without eggs or dairy. It is moist, rich, and delicious.

3 C flour
1 tsp. baking powder
1 tsp. baking soda
¼ tsp. salt
2½ Tbl. poppy seeds (do not purchase seeds from the bulk dept.)
1¼ C sugar
1/3 C vegetable oil
3 Tbl. water, 3 Tbl. oil, 2 tsp. baking powder; mixed together
1¼ C water
¼ C FRESH lemon juice
2 tsp. vanilla
1 tsp. grated lemon peel

Preheat oven to 350 degrees. Spray Bundt pan with dairy-free cooking spray.

Whisk together flour, baking powder, baking soda, salt, and poppy seeds. Set aside.

Combine sugar and oil in a large bowl; beat well. Add water/oil/baking powder mixture, water, lemon juice and vanilla; thoroughly combine.

Add dry ingredients to the wet ingredients and mix well.

Fold in lemon peel until completely incorporated. Pour batter into prepared Bundt pan.

Bake 43 minutes or until tester inserted in center comes out clean.

Cool in pan 10 minutes. Remove from pan and cool completely on a wire rack.

Upside-Down Fudge Cake

This easy cake is made with its own fudge frosting! Rich and chocolatey, it is a sure hit with the bib-wearing (required!) crew.

1 C flour
¼ tsp. salt
1 tsp. baking powder
1½ Tbl. unsweetened cocoa powder
2 Tbl. dairy-free margarine
¾ C sugar
½ C water
Topping (see below)

Preheat oven to 350 degrees. Grease a 9-inch square pan.

Whisk together the flour, salt, baking powder, and cocoa. Set aside.

In a large, glass bowl melt the margarine. Add sugar and water and thoroughly combine.

Add dry ingredients to the wet ingredients and stir well. Pour into prepared pan.

Topping:
½ C sugar
½ C brown sugar
¼ C unsweetened cocoa powder
1¼ C boiling water

Combine sugars and cocoa. Sprinkle evenly over dough. Pour boiling water evenly over mixture in pan.

Bake cake for 30 minutes. Let cool in pan.

A fudge frosting is created on the bottom of the cake. To serve, scoop out a slice and invert it onto a serving plate.

Chocolate Banana Cake Bars

These bars are very moist and rich with just a hint of banana.

1½ C flour
1 tsp. baking powder
1 tsp. baking soda
½ tsp. salt
1/3 C unsweetened cocoa powder
½ C dairy-free margarine
1¼ C sugar
1 tsp. vanilla
1½ Tbl. water, 1½ Tbl. oil, 1 tsp. baking powder; mixed together
1½ C mashed ripe bananas (about 3 medium)
1 C dairy-free, nut-free chocolate chips

Preheat oven to 350 degrees. Grease a 9-inch x 13-inch baking pan.

Whisk the flour, baking powder, baking soda, salt, and cocoa powder. Set aside.

In a large, glass bowl melt the margarine. Add sugar and beat until fluffy. Add vanilla and water/oil/baking powder mixture; beat until thoroughly combined. Blend in the bananas.

Add dry ingredients to the wet ingredients and mix well.

Fold in chocolate chips.

Pour into prepared baking pan.

Bake for 25 minutes, or until tester comes out clean. Cut into bars to serve.

Kingma's Favorite Chocolate Cupcakes

I present to you our favorite cupcakes. This easy recipe will delight your whole family for years to come!

Cake:
3 C flour
2 C sugar
½ C unsweetened cocoa powder
2 tsp. baking soda
1 tsp. salt
2 C cold water
1 C canola oil
1 Tbl. vanilla
1 ½ C dairy-free, nut-free, semi-sweet chocolate chips

Preheat oven to 350 degrees. Prepare muffin tin with paper liners.

Whisk flour, sugar, cocoa powder, baking soda, and salt in a large bowl. Set aside.

In a separate large bowl, combine water, oil, and vanilla.

Whisk dry ingredients into the wet ingredients until blended.

Fill muffin cups about 2/3 full. Sprinkle chocolate chips over each cupcake.

Bake for about 17 minutes, or until tester comes out clean.

Frosting:
½ C + 2 Tbl. dairy-free margarine
5 C confectioners' sugar
8 Tbl. soymilk (plain or vanilla) (adjust for good consistency)
1¼ tsp. vanilla
¾ C + 3 Tbl. unsweetened cocoa powder

In a large glass bowl melt the margarine. Add sugar, soymilk, vanilla, and cocoa; beat until creamy and smooth. Frost cooled cupcakes.

Pineapple Upside-Down Cake

This dairy-free, egg-free version of this old fashioned cake is delicious. My boys go crazy for the topping.

Topping:
2 Tbl. dairy-free margarine
1/3 C brown sugar
1 Tbl. water
1 (8-ounce) can sliced pineapple, drained and cut in half
maraschino cherries (optional)

Cake:
1 1/3 C flour
2/3 C sugar
2 tsp. baking powder
¼ C dairy-free margarine
2/3 C soymilk: vanilla or plain
1½ Tbl. water, 1½ Tbl. oil, 1 tsp. baking powder; mixed together
1 tsp. vanilla

Preheat oven to 350 degrees.

Topping: Melt the margarine and pour into a 9-inch round baking pan. Stir in brown sugar and water. Arrange the pineapple slices (and maraschino cherries if using) evenly around pan.

Cake: Whisk together flour, sugar, and baking powder. Set aside.

Melt margarine in a large glass bowl. Stir in soymilk, water/oil/baking powder mixture, and vanilla until combined.

Add dry ingredients to wet ingredients and mix well.

Pour cake batter evenly over the pineapple slices.

Bake for 30 to 35 minutes, until tester comes out clean. Cool on wire rack for 5 minutes.

Run a knife around edges of pan and invert cake onto a serving plate.

White Cake

This pleasing cake has great taste and great texture. It is perfect for birthday cakes or special occasion cakes.

3 C flour
2 C sugar
2 tsp. baking soda
1 tsp. salt
¾ C canola oil
2 tsp. vanilla
2 C water
2 Tbl. white vinegar

Preheat oven to 350 degrees. Grease and flour two 9-inch round baking pans.

Whisk together the flour, sugar, baking soda, and salt in a large bowl. Set aside.

Whisk together the oil, vanilla, and water. Add wet ingredients to the dry ingredients and stir until well blended.

Add white vinegar and quickly stir until thoroughly incorporated.

Pour batter into prepared cake pans.

Bake for 25 to 30 minutes, until tester inserted in the center comes out clean.

Cool in pans for 10 minutes. Invert cakes onto wire rack to cool completely.

Heirloom Applesauce Cake

A hearty, moist snack cake is grand enough for a party, sturdy enough for backpacking. Wrapped pieces hold up well in the freezer. This is from my dear friend Nancy Grayum.

6 - 8 fresh apples (3½ cups applesauce)
2 C sugar
½ C shortening
3 C flour
¼ to 1 tsp. cloves (to taste)
1 tsp. cinnamon
1 tsp. allspice
1 tsp. salt
1 tsp. baking powder
3½ tsp. baking soda

Peel and slice apples. Place into a large saucepan with a splash of water and cook down to a sauce. The consistency should not be too smooth, just cook until all the apple pieces are soft; stir constantly.

Preheat oven to 350 degrees.

Remove apples from heat. Measure to be sure of quantity, then place the 3½ cups applesauce back into the pan.

Add sugar, then shortening. Stir until shortening is melted.

In a separate bowl, whisk together flour, cloves, cinnamon, allspice, salt, baking powder and baking soda.

Add dry ingredients to applesauce, stirring thoroughly.

Pour mixture into a 9-inch x 13-inch glass baking dish.

Bake for about 45 minutes, until tester comes out clean.

From Nancy Grayum, via: Mom/Gwen Weiser Grayum, Grandma/Elsie Hansen Weiser, Great Grandma/Mary Tate Hansen. Original recipe included 1 C nuts, perhaps someday we can add them!

GOODIES

Chocolate Pudding

This dairy-free and egg-free pudding tastes and feels like the real (dairy-laden) thing! Delectable! I hope your family enjoys this treat as much as our family does!

1 C sugar
1/3 C unsweetened cocoa powder
5 Tbl. cornstarch
¼ tsp. salt
3 C water
1 Tbl. dairy-free margarine
1 tsp. vanilla

Whisk together sugar, cocoa powder, cornstarch, and salt in a large saucepan.

Add water, stirring with the whisk until well combined.

Bring to a boil over medium heat. Boil one minute, stirring constantly. Remove from heat.

Add margarine and vanilla and stir until completely incorporated. Pudding should be thick and smooth.

Pour into individual glass bowls/cups. Let cool to room temperature.

Chill completely in the refrigerator before serving.

Raspberry Shortbread Bars

These quick and easy bars are a sweet hit with everybody. The shortbread base mixed with coconut and raspberry is a delight to the senses.

1½ C flour
3/4 C sugar
1 tsp. baking powder
1 C dairy-free margarine
1½ C oats
½ C sweetened flaked coconut
raspberry preserves
dairy-free, nut-free chocolate chips (optional)
extra coconut (optional)

Preheat oven to 350 degrees. Grease 8-inch by 8-inch baking pan.

Whisk together flour, sugar, and baking powder in a large bowl. Cut in margarine with a pastry blender.

Add oats and coconut; mix until crumbly.

Press half of mixture into prepared pan. Spread raspberry preserves over the bottom mixture, using enough jelly for even coverage. Sprinkle remaining crumb mixture over raspberry layer.

Top with additional coconut and chocolate chips if desired.

Bake 25-30 minutes or until lightly browned. Center may seem soft.

Cool completely in pan on wire rack. Refrigerate two hours before serving to set this treat (IF you can wait).

Tasty Pumpkin Bars

These taste like pumpkin pie and my boys go crazy over them! The texture is perfect in these irresistible bars.

Topping:
¼ C cornstarch
¾ C firmly packed brown sugar
1 (.25-ounce) packet unflavored gelatin
1 tsp. cinnamon
¼ tsp. nutmeg
¼ tsp. ginger
1 (15 ounce) can pureed pumpkin
2 C egg-free mini-marshmallows (divided)

Crust:
½ C dairy-free margarine
1¼ C crushed dairy-free, nut-free graham cracker crumbs

Preheat oven to 350 degrees.

In a large bowl whisk together cornstarch, brown sugar, gelatin, cinnamon, nutmeg and ginger until smooth.

Stir in pumpkin, blending thoroughly. Fold in 1 C mini-marshmallows. Set aside.

To prepare crust: Melt margarine in a medium glass bowl. Stir in graham cracker crumbs until combined.

Pat crust into an 8-inch x 8-inch baking dish. Top with remaining 1 C mini-marshmallows and place in oven for 5 minutes until marshmallows melt. Remove from oven and spread melted marshmallow cream evenly over the crust.

Spread pumpkin mixture over melted marshmallows and bake for an additional 30 minutes.

Remove from oven and cool completely. Refrigerate until set.

Brownies

This is our favorite brownie. I tried many recipes, as a "safe" brownie was my personal quest when I was still breastfeeding and had to strictly abide by the food rules. They are chewy, rich, and decadent, just like a "real" brownie should be.

1¾ C flour
½ C unsweetened cocoa powder
1 C sugar
1½ tsp. baking soda
¼ C vegetable oil
½ C water
1/3 C light corn syrup
1 tsp. vanilla
1½ tsp. white vinegar
1 C dairy-free, nut-free chocolate chips
topping: confectioners' sugar or egg-free mini marshmallows

Preheat oven to 350 degrees. Grease an 8-inch x 8-inch baking pan.

Whisk together flour, cocoa powder, sugar, and baking soda. Set aside.

In a large bowl, combine the oil, water, corn syrup, vanilla, and vinegar, blending thoroughly.

Add dry ingredients to the wet ingredients and stir well.

Fold in the chocolate chips.

Spread evenly into prepared pan.

Bake for 20 to 25 minutes, until tester comes out clean.

For topping, sift confectioners' sugar evenly over the top or sprinkle marshmallows evenly over the top of the baked brownies.

Crispy Rice Goodies

These treats are the kid-pleasing stand-by that is simple to adapt to dairy-free.

3 Tbl. dairy-free margarine
1 pkg. (10 oz.) or about 40 large egg-free marshmallows or 4 C egg-free mini-marshmallows
6 C nut-free, dairy-free, crunchy rice cereal

Grease a 9-inch x 13-inch baking pan. Set aside.

Melt margarine in large non-stick saucepan over low heat. Add marshmallows and stir until marshmallows are completely melted and incorporated.

Remove from heat and stir in cereal until well coated.

Press evenly in prepared baking pan.

Use a greased spatula or hands, or waxed paper to pat the mixture into the pan for greatest ease.

Homemade Popsicles!

Safe, easy, super-fun Popsicles add sparkle to any warm day.

Juice—your favorite selection
Molds
Freezer

There are many varieties of Popsicle molds available. My kids do not seem to care about what juice they are made from, so I use 100% real juice.

First, pour the juice into the molds and then insert the handle topper. Place level in the freezer. When they are frozen, fill a medium bowl with warm water and set the mold into the water for a few seconds. The frozen formed Popsicles should slide out easily.

Yogurt Cups

These are so fun, so yummy, and so easy! The basic shortbread "cup" can be filled with anything that delights your child. We've filled the cups with soy yogurts, jelly, and even fruit. Double the recipe so you can eat some!

¼ C dairy-free margarine
¾ C flour
3 Tbl. confectioners' sugar
2 to 3 tsp. cold water
1½ C soy yogurt, or filling

Preheat the oven to 375 degrees.

In a large glass bowl melt the margarine. Mix in flour and sugar until crumbly; sprinkle in water, 1 tsp. at a time, stirring until dough is formed.

Drop about 1 Tbl. of dough into ungreased mini muffin tins. Press down with a tart shaper (or equivalent) to make a nice "cup."

Bake until golden brown, about 11 minutes. Let cool in the tin at least 10 minutes.

Carefully remove cups from tins with a spatula; let cool completely on wire rack.

Fill with your favorite soy yogurt, sugared strawberries, apple pie filling (homemade or "safe" canned versions). This is a great dessert to share with a party.

Fruit Smoothies

Fruit smoothies are an easy and tasty way to get your kids to "eat" fruit. I constantly experiment, using the fruits that I have handy, always using bananas and soymilk as a base. Use your imagination, or better yet, let your kids concoct their own versions.

3 bananas
½ to 1 C soymilk: plain or flavored
½ C crushed ice
A handful of washed, de-stemmed and de-skinned fruit: strawberries, raspberries, blackberries, kiwi, blueberries, mango, etc. I like to use frozen fruit, for a slushy-feel.
Other possible additions: soy yogurt, tofu, and wheat bran

Combine your selection of ingredients and puree in a blender until smooth. Enjoy immediately with straws!

Easy Holiday Dairy-free Fudge

I'm partial to the easy-preparation fudge. Here is a great dairy-free version of the fun holiday treat!

6 Tbl. dairy-free margarine
1/4 C soymilk (plain or vanilla)
3½ C confectioners' sugar
½ C unsweetened cocoa powder
1 tsp. vanilla
Additions/Toppings: sweetened, flaked coconut, chopped up "safe" peppermint sticks, mini-marshmallows, candied red cherry pieces

Grease loaf pan (5-inch by 9-inch bread pan). If you wish, you can coat the bottom with a chosen topping.

Melt margarine in the top of a double boiler. Add soymilk, confectioners' sugar, cocoa powder, and vanilla. Mix over simmering water until very smooth. Remove from heat.

Stir in a chosen addition, if you desire. Pour mixture into prepared pan. Chill and cut into small squares.

Popcorn Balls

This 'flashback from my childhood' snack is quite a hit with my children. It is messy to make, but so fun and yummy to eat. Make it a year-round, joint-effort treat.

9 to 10 C popped natural popcorn (air popped in your machine)
¾ C brown sugar, packed
¼ C water or apple juice
3 Tbl. dairy-free margarine
2 Tbl. corn syrup
¼ tsp. salt
1 C raisins
1 C dried cranberries

Grease a large bowl with dairy-free margarine. Place popped popcorn and dried fruit into the greased bowl.

Combine sugar, juice or water, margarine, corn syrup, and salt in a large saucepan. Boil over medium heat for 5 to 6 minutes, stirring, until thickened.

Drizzle hot mixture over the popcorn, stirring quickly.

Create 4-inch balls with margarine-coated hands and place on large platter.

Let cool and harden before eating.

Blackberry Pie

My husband is the pie baker in our household and the boys await blackberry season with great anticipation. This pie is a perfect summer dessert.

Pastry:
2 C flour
½ tsp. salt
2/3 C vegetable shortening
6 to 7 Tbl. cold water

Whisk together the flour and salt. Cut in the shortening with a pastry blender until the dough is crumbly and the size of peas.

Add one tablespoon of cold water at a time and mix in with a fork. When a uniform dough is formed, divide in half.

On a floured surface, roll out one of the dough halves to about a 12-inch diameter. Place on the bottom of a 9-inch diameter pie pan. Fill with prepared blackberries (directions following). Roll out the remaining dough to about a 12-inch diameter. Place on top of pie filling. Crimp the edges together and cut a few slits across the top.

Cover the edges with foil and bake in a 350 degree oven for 50 minutes. Remove foil and bake for an additional 20 to 30 minutes, until the crust is golden and the berries are tender.

Blackberry Filling:
½ C sugar
¼ C flour
4 C ripe blackberries, cleaned and sorted

Combine sugar and flour in a large bowl. Add berries and toss well to coat berries evenly.

Peach Cobbler

This dessert brings back great childhood memories for me. My boys love it as much as I do. Summer goodness and sweetness emanate from this delightful, easy dessert.

4 pounds ripe peaches, peeled, pitted, and cut into ½-inch slices (thawed frozen peaches may be used)
1 C sugar, divided
¼ C quick-cooking tapioca
1½ tsp. grated lemon peel
1½ Tbl. lemon juice (fresh is best)
1½ tsp. vanilla
2 C flour
1¼ tsp. baking powder
11 Tbl. dairy-free margarine, cut into chunks
2/3 C plain or vanilla soymilk
dairy-free cooking spray

In a large bowl, combine peaches, 2/3 C sugar, tapioca, lemon peel, lemon juice, and vanilla. Let stand for about 30 minutes, stirring occasionally.

Preheat oven to 350 degrees. Grease a 3-quart baking dish.

In a separate large bowl, whisk together 1/3 C sugar, flour, and baking powder. Cut in margarine with a pastry blender until the mixture looks like coarse crumbs. Stir in soymilk just until dough holds together.

Spread the fruit evenly on the bottom of prepared dish. Drop dough by tablespoons over the top of the fruit, spreading with two spoons, so all the filling is covered.

Bake for 50 to 60 minutes, until top is golden brown and the fruit mixture bubbles. I suggest placing a cookie sheet on the rack below the baking dish to catch drips.

Apple Crisp

My family cannot get enough of the deliciously crispy topping on this delectable baked treat.

2 Tbl. dairy-free margarine, for greasing the casserole dish
4 C apples, thinly sliced
1 tsp. cinnamon
½ C water
½ C dairy-free margarine
1 C sugar
¾ C flour

Preheat oven to 400 degrees. Generously grease an 8-inch x 11-inch baking dish with the 2 Tbl. margarine.

Place sliced apples evenly over the bottom of the dish. Whisk cinnamon and water together. Pour evenly over the apples.

In a medium glass bowl, melt the ½ C margarine. Add sugar and flour and mix with a pastry blender until the dough is the size of peas. Spread evenly over the apple mixture.

Bake for 30 to 45 minutes, or until topping is golden brown and the apple mixture is bubbly.

Spider Web Chocolates

This novelty is easy to make and makes a great impression on the kids. Who needs Halloween chocolate candy when they can have a chocolate spider web?

dairy-free, nut-free, black licorice sticks (or can use straight "safe" pretzels)
dairy-free, nut-free, semi-sweet chocolate chips
Wax paper

Place wax paper on the countertop.

Cut licorice into 4-inch sections. On the wax paper, arrange two licorice sections to make an "X." Place an additional licorice stick horizontally across the middle of the "X."

Melt chocolate chips in a Ziploc sandwich bag in the microwave. Cut a SMALL hole in one corner of the bag.

First, "glue" the licorice sticks together with the melted chocolate. Carefully squeeze chocolate in a spider web fashion: connecting the licorice sections with thin ribbons of chocolate. After a strand is completely woven around the licorice foundation, begin another one. Continue to the outer edge. It should look like a spider web.

Let chocolate completely harden. This should take at least a couple of hours.

If the curiosity overcomes your child and they try to pick it up, remind them it is very fragile until completely hardened. I let my kids suck out the remaining chocolate in the sandwich bag to satisfy their urge.

I hope your costumed kids enjoy this special treat!

"Halleluiah, It's Ice Cream Time!" Soy Ice Cream

Here is the answer from heaven: homemade ice cream using soymilk and soy lecithin for perfect texture and perfect taste. Grab your coffee cans, its time to rock and roll.

1½ C soymilk (vanilla or plain)
¾ C frozen or fresh fruit: strawberries are divine!
½ C sugar
1/8 C canola oil
½ Tbl. liquid soy lecithin (found in the supplements section/expensive, but worth it!)
½ tsp. vanilla
dash of salt
crushed ice and rock salt for the coffee can procedure

Slice fruit. Place fruit and soymilk in blender. Pulsate until blended.

Add sugar, canola oil, soy lecithin, vanilla, and salt. Blend until smooth.

Place mixture in an ice cream maker and follow manufacturer's directions. You can double the recipe.

Or:
Place mixture in a 1-pound coffee can with a tight fitting lid (I have also used a large, plastic yogurt container). Duct tape the lid, so it is watertight.

Place the sealed 1-pound container in a 3-pound coffee can with a tight fitting lid. Pack crushed ice around the smaller can. Pour at least ¾ C of rock salt evenly over the ice.

Place lid on the 3-pound can. Roll the prepared can back and forth on a hard surface for about 10 minutes.

Open outer can. Remove inner can and remove lid. Use a spatula and thoroughly stir the forming ice cream. Replace lid. Drain any melted ice from the outer can and add more crushed ice and rock salt, as needed. Roll back and forth for an additional 5-10 minutes. Open cans, serve immediately, and hear your little angels sing!

Chocolate Chunks

These chocolate chunks are easy to make and a lifesaver
when you are unable to find dairy-free, nut-free chocolate
chips that are essential in life. You can also create safe
chocolate bars for your child with this recipe.

1 (8 ounce) package of dairy-free, nut-free unsweetened
baking chocolate (yes-use all 8 1-ounce bars)
¼ C, plus 1 tsp. shortening
1/8 tsp. vanilla
2 C confectioners' sugar

Break the chocolate into chunks. Melt chocolate chunks and
the shortening in a large glass bowl in the microwave until the
chocolate is melted.

Stir until smooth. Add vanilla and combine.

Stir in confectioners' sugar one cup at a time until blended.
Knead mixture until sugar is completely incorporated and
mixture is smooth.

Spread chocolate mixture into pans. For chocolate chunks,
spread mixture into two 11-inch by 8-inch pans.

Option: Spread half of the mixture thinly in an 11-inch by 8-
inch pan for chunks and then spread the other half, in a bit
thicker layer, in an 8-inch by 8-inch pan, top with "safe"
baking sprinkles and create chocolate "bars."

Cover pans and refrigerate until firm. Break into desired
pieces. Store in the refrigerator.

This takes some energy—but it is worth it to have safe
chocolate chips on hand for your little one!

Pumpkin Pie Tarts

Autumn tarts make everyone smile. These taste like the real pie.

Crust:
½ C dairy-free margarine
1½ C flour
6 Tbl. confectioners' sugar
4 to 5 tsp. cold water

Filling:
1/8 C cornstarch
¼ C firmly packed brown sugar
Half of a (1-ounce) packet unflavored gelatin
½ tsp. ground cinnamon
1/8 tsp. ground nutmeg
1/8 tsp. ground ginger
1 C pureed pumpkin
1 C egg-free mini-marshmallows

Preheat the oven to 375 degrees.

Crust: In a large glass bowl melt the margarine. Mix in flour and sugar until crumbly; sprinkle in water, 1 tsp. at a time, stirring until dough is formed.

Drop about 1 Tbl. of dough into ungreased mini muffin tins. Press down with a tart shaper (or equivalent) to make a nice "cup."

Filling: In a large bowl whisk together cornstarch, brown sugar, gelatin, cinnamon, nutmeg and ginger until smooth. Stir in pumpkin, blending thoroughly. Fold in mini-marshmallows.

Spoon filling into cups, being sure to include at least a couple of mini-marshmallows in each compartment.

Bake for 11 minutes.

Turn oven down to 325 degrees. Bake for an additional 7 minutes, or until tester comes out clean. Top each with an additional mini-marshmallow.

Oatmeal Jelly Bars

These super quick bars are a fast solution for a sweet tooth.

1 C flour
1 C oats
2/3 C brown sugar
¼ tsp. baking soda
½ C dairy-free margarine
Jelly—homemade or a safe variety

Preheat oven to 350 degrees.

Whisk flour, oats, brown sugar, and baking soda together in a large bowl.

Cut in margarine with a pastry blender until mixture resembles coarse crumbs.

Reserve ½ C oatmeal mixture. Press remaining dough into the bottom of an ungreased 9-inch x 9-inch baking pan.

Spread with your choice of safe jelly. Sprinkle the remaining oat mixture evenly over the top.

Bake for 30 to 35 minutes, until topping is golden brown.

SNACKS

Ideas

The following snack ideas have served my family well these past years. I strive to provide safe, nutritious, delicious snacks to my two growing, young boys. I hope to inspire some good dairy-free, egg-free, nut-free reliable ideas for you to use in your snack repertoire.

**Fruit: My boys are HUGE fruit eaters and I like to surprise them with out-of-season fruits to keep them interested. I give them total access to the fruit bowl.

** Cereals: dairy-free, egg-free, nut-free varieties. We enjoy safe cereals on their own, or mixed together with mini-marshmallows, raisins, dried cranberries, "safe" chocolate chips, etc.

**Air popped popcorn: We LOVE to watch the action with our home air-popper. We like to eat it (supervised with young ones, of course!) with a sprinkle of seasoned salt on top.

**Edamames: young soybeans in the pod or without. I always have a frozen bag in the freezer. Boil them according to the manufacturer's directions, and serve them warm with sea salt sprinkled on top for a very tasty and very healthy treat.

**Jell-O: either gloppy, or finger-style. What kid doesn't like Jell-O? I love to cut out star shapes for finger-styled special snack time; it's a sure thing!

**Bugs: whole wheat Ritz-style cracker, topped with soy-nut butter and raisins. This is one of our favorite snacks! Works with celery too!

**Graham crackers: I've found that the main brands are to be more trusted than store brands. Add soy margarine atop for an even yummier treat.

Worms: (can you tell that I mother boys?) "safe," packaged, deli-style meat, cut into strips (avoid "sliced at the deli" meats—the slicing machine is used for cutting the cheeses as well)

Cracker sandwiches: whole-wheat Ritz crackers as "bread" with a piece of deli meat as filling

** **Pretzels**: any and all shapes. Check the ingredients! Stick with the major brands, as some pretzels are made on equipment with peanuts.

Fruit leather: My boys adore fruit leather and I occasionally indulge them. I always check the ingredients and watch for "made on equipment with peanuts!" I have found that many fruit <u>snacks</u> are made on equipment with peanuts, so we avoid them.

Good ole saltine crackers: "squares" as we call them (watch for dairy ingredients/stick to main brands).

Wheat-Thin-type crackers: I don't often get them, so they are a special treat. Again, stick to major brands to avoid "made on equipment with nuts."

Soy yogurts: there are many delicious varieties. My kids love to add Grape-Nuts cereal for a crunchy treat.

Applesauce: grandma often brings homemade applesauce for the kids. We have also found tubes of applesauce (similar to the yogurt tubes) that my kids ADORE!

Veggies: my boys will go for thinly sliced carrots, celery, and red peppers. They will eat them for sure if I have hummus for dipping.

** **Smoked Salmon**: My boys are huge fish eaters and devour smoked salmon like crazy!! We usually eat Grandpa's smoked salmon, but there are safe varieties that you buy.

Dried fruit (thinly sliced): any and all varieties.

Pepperoni Roll Ups

This is one of our favorite snacks AND a quick and easy lunch. When you microwave the pepperoni, it leaks some tasty juice that permeates the tortilla and makes it extra tasty.

8 to 10 slices dairy-free pepperoni slices
1 flour tortilla (size is optional)

Line up the pepperoni slices in a row near one edge of the tortilla, and roll up, pressing to make sure it stays together.

Microwave 33 seconds on HIGH in the microwave. Let cool slightly and eat OVER the plate, as it tends to drip.

Meat Roll Ups

This is Evan's all-time favorite lunch and snack. I'm telling you--I won't be caught dead without some soy-cream cheese in the house in case he gets a hankering.

1 slice dairy-free, preferred packaged deli meat
1 good smear of soy-cream cheese substitute

Smear a good dab a tofu cream cheese in a line near the bottom of the slice of meat. Roll up meat. Pat a dab of cream cheese on the end flap, roll into the meat roll and press, so it stays together.

Fun Time Granola Bars

These bars are so tasty; they will outscore the packaged varieties any day!

½ C flour
½ C whole-wheat flour
1 tsp. cornstarch
1 tsp. cinnamon
1 tsp. baking powder
½ C dairy-free margarine
1 C firmly packed brown sugar
1/3 C sugar
2 Tbl. honey
1 tsp. vanilla
1½ C oats
¼ C "safe" wheat germ
1 C nut-free, dairy-free, egg-free crispy rice cereal
1 C raisins
1 C dairy-free, nut-free chocolate chips/chunks
2/3 C egg-free mini-marshmallows

Preheat oven to 350 degrees. Grease a 9-inch x 13-inch baking pan.

Whisk together flours, cornstarch, cinnamon, and baking powder. Set aside.

In a large, glass bowl melt the margarine. Beat in sugars until fluffy. Add honey and vanilla and combine.

Add dry ingredients to wet ingredients and mix well. Fold in oats, wheat germ, cereal, raisins, and chocolate chips until combined.

Pat dough into the prepared pan. Sprinkle mini-marshmallows evenly over the top.

Bake for 20 minutes until golden brown. Cool completely and cut into bars.

"Even Healthier" Granola Bars

These bars are delicious and jam-packed full of "hidden" nutrition.

½ C flour
½ C whole-wheat flour
1 tsp. cornstarch
1 tsp. cinnamon
1 tsp. baking powder
½ C dairy-free margarine
2/3 C firmly packed brown sugar
2 Tbl. sugar
1/3 C honey
1 tsp. vanilla
1¼ C oats
¼ C "safe" wheat germ
¼ C flax seed (freshly ground up in a clean coffee grinder)
1 C nut-free, dairy-free, egg-free crispy rice cereal
1C raisins
1 C dried cranberries
small handful of egg-free mini-marshmallows

Preheat oven to 350 degrees. Grease a 9-inch x 13-inch baking pan.

Whisk together flours, cornstarch, cinnamon, and baking powder. Set aside.

In a large, glass bowl melt the margarine. Add sugars and beat until fluffy. Blend in honey and vanilla.

Add dry ingredients to wet ingredients and mix well. Fold in oats, wheat germ, flax seed, rice cereal, raisins, and cranberries until well mixed.

Pat dough into prepared pan. Sprinkle marshmallows over the top.

Bake for 20 minutes until golden brown. Cool completely and cut into bars.

Seasoned Cereal Snack Mix

We all love this special party food. No one can tell it is made with soy margarine and so is the perfect snack for parties.

2 Tbl. Worcestershire sauce
6 Tbl. dairy-free margarine
1½ tsp. seasoned salt
¾ tsp. garlic powder
½ tsp. onion powder
3 C nut-free, dairy-free, egg-free Corn Squares cereal
3 C nut-free, dairy-free, egg-free Rice Squares cereal
3 C nut-free, dairy-free, egg-free Wheat Squares cereal
1 C nut-free, dairy-free pretzels (stick to major brands!)
1 C nut-free, dairy-free, egg-free bagel chips, broken into pieces

Heat oven to 250 degrees.

Melt margarine in large roasting pan in oven, covering the bottom evenly. Stir in seasonings. Gradually stir in remaining ingredients until evenly coated.

Bake 1 hour, stirring every 15 minutes. Cool on paper towels.

Quesadillas

A delicious, healthy treat that is often requested at my house!

1-2 slices of VEGAN (completely dairy free!) cheese substitute slices
1 dairy-free, egg-free, nut-free tortilla

Place tortilla in oven. Turn oven on to 350 degrees. Flip tortilla over after about three minutes. Bake in heating oven for another three minutes, or until tortilla is lightly browned.

Tear vegan cheese substitute slices in strips and arrange around the warmed and crispy tortilla to cover completely.

Microwave on High for about 35 seconds, until melted. Tear or cut into triangles, let cool, and enjoy!

Hummus

This is one of our favorite snacks. It is a great way to "cover" vegetables one day. Just set out a bowl of hummus and some "safe" wheat crackers or thinly sliced vegetables for snack when they are really hungry.

2 medium cloves garlic, diced
1-1½ Tbl. of dried parsley
¼ C red onion, diced
2 (15 ½ -oz. cans) garbanzo beans, rinsed and well drained
6 Tbl. tahini (sesame paste; found in health food sections)
6 Tbl. fresh lemon juice
3/4 to 1 tsp. salt (to taste)
pinch of cumin (to taste)

Mince garlic, red onion, and parsley in a food processor or blender.

Gradually add garbanzo beans, tahini, lemon juice, and salt, and puree to a thick paste.

Season to taste with the cumin. Transfer to a tightly lidded container and chill.

Use it as a dip for "safe" crackers or thinly sliced, raw vegetables.

**I often just throw all the ingredients (first mincing the vegetables) in a bowl and mash it like crazy. It makes it thick and chunky and we like it that way, although some children would balk at this texture.

Eggplant Dip

This dip is great for crackers or thinly sliced, raw vegetables.
The kids don't even know that it is healthy.

1 medium (7-inch) eggplant
2 medium cloves garlic, minced
¼ C fresh lemon juice
¼ C tahini (sesame paste, found in health food sections)
½ tsp. salt
black pepper (to taste)

Preheat oven to 350 degrees. Grease a baking sheet.

Slice the eggplant in half lengthwise, and place facedown on
the baking sheet. Bake for 30 minutes, or until very tender.
Cool until it is comfortable to handle.

Scoop out the eggplant pulp and discard the skin. Place the
pulp in a food processor or blender. Add garlic, lemon juice,
tahini, and salt. Puree until smooth. Or mash by hand for a
chunkier version.

You can serve drizzled with olive oil and freshly minced
parsley on top.

Enjoy with "safe" crackers or thinly sliced, raw vegetables.

Dairy-Free, Nut-Free, Kid Pleasing Granola

In my everlasting quest for healthy snacks, this one really hits the mark. This granola is tasty, stays fresh for a good week, and is jam-packed full of the "good stuff."

½ C toasted, shredded coconut (sweetened or unsweetened)
4 C oats
¼ C "safe" wheat germ
3 Tbl. packaged sesame seeds (do not buy bulk/shared equipment with nuts!)
½ tsp. cinnamon
¼ tsp. freshly grated nutmeg (it makes a difference to do it fresh!)
½ C honey
8 Tbl. dairy-free margarine
½ C raisins

Preheat oven to 350 degrees.

Place the coconut in a single layer on a cookie sheet and toast until lightly browned. Set aside.

Lower the oven temperature to 300 degrees.

Combine the oats, wheat germ, sunflower seeds, sesame seeds, cinnamon, and nutmeg in a large bowl.

Melt the margarine in a separate glass bowl. Add honey and stir well.

Pour margarine mixture over the oat mixture and mix well.

Spread granola in a single layer on two cookie sheets. Bake for 20 minutes, or until golden.

After cooling, sprinkle in the raisins and toasted coconut. Store in a Ziploc bag.

Enjoy in a snack cup, or as a cereal with soymilk.

Creamy Bean Dip for Chips

This adaptation of an easy college favorite delights Evan. Use this recipe instead of nacho cheese for dip as hearty as a meal.

1 (15-ounce) can of "safe" chili: any dairy free variety
1 small tub of soy cream cheese substitute

In a small saucepan, stir together the chili and soy cream cheese until thoroughly combined and heated through.

Serve with "safe" tortilla chips.

Dairy-free, Egg-free Ranch Dip for Vegetables

I was excited to find a dairy-free Ranch spice packet. Now my boys can dip their "naked" carrots and eat twice as much!

Follow the spice packet's directions, adding soy sour cream substitute as the mixing medium for dipping delight. This dip can work as any ranch dipping for chips, chicken, or vegetables.

SUBSTITUTIONS

I have found the following substitutions to be particularly useful in various situations and circumstances while cooking or baking.

Dairy

Milk substitutions:
Soymilk: plain, vanilla, unsweetened, or flavored
Rice milk: plain or flavored
Water
Fruit juice: apple juice is particularly adaptable
Chicken broth (check for dairy and/or egg proteins!)
Vegetable broth (check for dairy and/or egg proteins!)
Beef broth (check for dairy and/or egg proteins!)

Make your own buttermilk substitution:

2/3 C soymilk: plain or unsweetened
1 ¼ C water
2 Tbl. dairy-free margarine

Combine all ingredients in a saucepan. Heat gently until the margarine is melted. Remove. Pour into a blender and blend until liquid turns creamy white (about 1 minute). Keep covered in the refrigerator and use within a couple of days.

Butter or dairy margarine substitutions:
Dairy-free margarine (I prefer soy margarines)
olive oil--use ¾ of the amount needed in a baking recipe
Vegetable oil (I prefer Canola Oil)--use ¾ amount needed in a recipe
vegetable shortening
lard

Cheese substitutions:
Minced tofu
Vegan cheese—made with no casein (check the label!)
Omit cheese entirely

Egg

Egg substitutions:
1½ Tbl. water, 1½ Tbl. oil, 1 tsp. baking powder; mixed together
      *my favorite for baking texture

1 Tbl. water, 1 Tbl. white vinegar, 1 tsp. baking powder; mixed together

1 Tbl. water, 1 Tbl. balsamic vinegar, 1 tsp. baking powder; mixed together

1-tsp. yeast dissolved in ¼ C warm water

1 packet unflavored gelatin dissolved in 2 Tbl. warm water

Helpful egg hints:
**add extra vanilla in baked goods for extra "oomph"
**add arrowroot powder or Xanthum Gum to baked goods to help the finished product avoid being so crumbly

Ground beef substitutions:
ground turkey--for less fat and calories
ground beef chuck
diced tofu: you'd be surprised and pleased with the favorable results
black beans

Chicken substitutions:
turkey chunks
tofu chunks
black beans

TIPS

I must admit that I am a bit of a natural worrywart. Couple that with having to be on constant food patrol and I do spend an inordinate amount of time obsessing about nutrition for my two small boys. It seems that "other" mothers can have their bases covered if their child drinks two glasses of milk and a couple of smears of peanut butter a day. We parents of food-allergic children have to have a more substantial and organized, militant approach to guaranteeing nutrition success. I am not a nutritionist and I know that vitamin enriched foods are not quite as powerful as whole foods, but hey--every little bit helps. Here are my tips, my game plan if you will, to assure myself of nutritional victory.

1)   **VITAMINS** Figure out what kind of vitamin your kids like best and stick with it, no matter what the cost. Finding a dairy-free selection is a somewhat perilous journey, but doable. My boys LOVE the Gummy Vites by L'Il Critters. They are in gummy bear form and taste like the real thing. I get them at Costco here. They may cost a bit more, but I'm positive that they take their vitamins each and every day.

2)   **JUICE** The only juice I have in the house is calcium fortified orange juice. They get great vitamins and the extra calcium and I let them drink it sparingly with snacks. I only allow water or milk with meals though--they need to fill up on good drinks.

3)   **SOYMILK** I always try to get the "PLUS" versions of the milk to get all the extra vitamins, protein and calcium. I was surprised that my boys actually like the plain flavor better than the vanilla. But whatever gets them to drink it, I go for it: hot cocoa, chocolate milk, with a straw, with mini marshmallows, whatever encourages them to drink more milk. Hershey's Chocolate Syrup is safe! I keep an eagle's eye on the sale ads each week for soymilk deals and really stock up when there is a sale, especially when I have corresponding coupons.
Continued:

SOYMILK/Continued

The best thing about soymilk is the incredible shelf life. Refrigerated soymilks are good--but I wouldn't say they score stellar taste points above the shelf variety. Of course, I stock up when they are on sale, but to tell you the truth, my boys don't really notice the difference. You also run the risk of spoilage with the refrigerated selections. My goal is to experience Evan outgrowing his dairy allergy BEFORE some of my shelf soymilk expires! It is very handy to have both plain and vanilla soymilk on hand for your baking and cooking needs. Scalloped potatoes just don't taste as good when made with vanilla soymilk! We have been drinking unsweetened lately.

4)   **SNACKS** Snacks are unavoidable in this snack obsessed culture. You will have to safely navigate your vulnerable child through a Goldfish cracker filled childhood. I carry snack cups with me wherever we go, in addition to safe crackers and/or homemade treats. It is always better to be over-prepared instead of ending up somewhere with no treat and no available easy alternatives. We snack on the different options I have listed in the "Snack section" and mostly on dairy-free, nut-free, vitamin enriched cereals. I buy a few different kinds of safe cereal and mix them up in a snack bowl with raisins, homemade granola, nut-free pretzels, etc. Again--the kids are getting extra vitamins and calcium from the enriched cereals.   Also, I have learned to carry a secret, extra special treat (lollipop or fruit leather in our case) for those few, inevitable times when Evan sees something that he wants and can't have. Nothing calms a screaming toddler like a special treat that no one else can have. We are also huge fruit eaters. They also really go for Hummus or an eggplant dip with "safe" crackers.

5)   **FOOD ALTERNATIVES** I want to rave about my favorite tofu products. Tofutti is a wonderful brand with Sour Supreme sour cream alternative, and Better than Cream Cheese cream cheese alternative. They taste and feel like the real thing! Evan's favorite lunch is "meat roll-ups" safe bologna rolled up with Tofutti Better than Cream Cheese inside. I.M. Healthy has both a crunchy and creamy Soy Nut Butter (peanut butter substitute) that tastes great.

Silk brand or Wholesoy yogurts are the best for taste and texture; Evan is a true fan. There are several soybean margarines available. I mostly use Shedd's Willow Run or Nucoa margarine (found in the general grocer margarine section). I am not so impressed with soy cheese selections. Be sure you check the ingredients. It is my experience that ONLY the cheeses marked VEGAN are dairy-free. Most of the cheeses labeled as "soy" have casein as one of the top ingredients. Your local Food Coop, Fred Meyer/Kroger Nutrition Center, or good grocery store should carry these products and more. Molly Katzen's <u>Moosewood Cookbook </u>has several egg-less mayonnaise recipes using tofu. You might find a good mayonnaise alternative.

6)   **FOOD PREP IDEAS** Stock up on mushrooms when they are in season and devote a couple of hours to making your own jumbo size Cream of Mushroom soup using soy margarine and soymilk (see Soups). Divvy up the batch into useable substitution portions; pour them into large, freezer zip lock bags and wha la! Freeze them flat in your freezer for optimum room and enjoy the convenience. Who needs mushroom soup in a can? Use for all of your favorite recipes calling for this soup.

Definitely make a double batch of your favorite meal and freeze half. You WILL have evenings when you don't have the time to cook. If you prepare ahead, you'll always be covered.

Use your bread machine! It is guaranteed safe and so much healthier for you and your family.

Don't skimp on the vanilla extract. Get the real stuff and use it! I always add just a touch more than what is called for, because I've found that using vanilla gives the baked goods some extra "oomph," especially in waffles and pancakes.

Like any mother, I secretly add minced vegetables to anything that I can and add wheat bran, wheat germ, and/or flax seed (freshly ground) to almost all of my baked goods. My new goal is to replace at least half of my regular flour with whole-wheat flour in my baking recipes AND to eat vegetarian once a week.

7) **SAFE PLACES** I have learned to be very selective about the places I am willing to bring Evan. I am worried about him picking up some interesting snack (read: Goldfish crackers) and plopping it into his mouth before I can stop him. I've barely taken my eyes off that child his entire babyhood, toddler hood, and racing into childhood. It is exhausting. So I pick and choose where we go. The library is definitely IN. I do find discarded snacks now and then, but generally it is clean. We are really lucky because our library is wonderful and has many reading group activities.

We also have participated in a "More Than One" Baby-N-Me class at the local technical college. I hand out a sheet at the beginning of each session describing Evan's allergies, with "Signifying milk, egg, and nut proteins" lists, as well as snack ideas. They have been great and supportive. It helps that they are a "nut-free" institution, so they are particularly aware of the food allergy issue.

Woods--we live in a great place and spend many an afternoon hiking and exploring in the woods around our house. It is enough for now. I encourage it as a healthy and brain broadening activity. If you add a homemade Popsicle, it doubles the pleasure and raises your stature to one of supreme loved mommy.

Beaches--is there anything better than sandy beaches for summer digging fun and rocky beaches for crab hunting and beach combing? Of course, keep an ever-vigilant eye out for littered snacks, which are occasionally present.

I have two kids--and things are definitely better now that they are older. But for a while I had to put on hold activities that got way beyond my control. We attended free gym time for a while. My older son would get into confrontations and I would have to divert my attention to him, leaving Evan vulnerable in that snack littered environment. So we quit going to that until the boys were older. Then Leighton handled himself better while Evan just wanted to battle over toys instead of searching for floor food.

Anything with tunnels is out--it is too hard to supervise. Those places (fast food restaurants, tube play places, children's museums, etc.) serve food--which of course can end up in those tunnels where you cannot watch your child.

Friends' houses--here we go: you soon learn who your friends are by their valiant housekeeping efforts yet you will still feel the stomach knots when your vulnerable child goes down to the playroom where food is not allowed. Because you never know--maybe just for one occasion they had cookies down there. There is nothing more uncomfortable than picking up some crumbs off the floor of someone else's house-especially in front of them. I usually talk my way to the room with my child, so I can supervise him nonstop. You pick your supportive friends and choose when to visit and when to insist with good cheer that they come visit you.

Parks are the biggest food pigsties around, according to my hypercritical observations. I do believe that caregivers carelessly discard leftover snacks thinking that birds will come along and eat all the bits and pieces that are littered around. These people do not realize that this offensive action can spell disaster for an allergic, curious child. We ONLY go to playgrounds with my husband, or a close, understanding friend, where we can divide and conquer. This situation calls for extreme diligence and is truthfully very stressful for me and I usually just go play in the woods instead.

8)   **RECOMMENDED BOOKS AND SUPPORT SYSTEMS**
It is a lonely thing to have a child with a life threatening food allergy. Acquaintances and family members disregard your life-and-death reality as being some "fad, hippy, and granola mommy thing." I have seen the eye rolling. I have been told to, "Stop this nonsense." I have kept my manners after ANOTHER family inquiry as to what Evan is allergic to, after politely declining the chocolate candy AGAIN. People don't have as much interest in your child as you do. Okay--I accept that, but it sure doesn't make for much of a social life.
Continued:

I turned to FAAN (The Food Allergy & Anaphylaxis Network: 10400 Eaton Place, Suite 107, Fairfax, VA 22030-2208, 1-800-929-4040, www.foodallergy.org) for support. They were far away and did not know me, but I counted on them. I felt camaraderie with the parents who wrote tales and tips. I highly recommend them as a perfect starting place. They have vast amounts of information, recipes, and cookbooks. It is a source of comfort to know that there are many parents out there in exactly the same boat as we are.

The Parent's Guide to Food Allergies: Clear and Complete Advice From the Experts on Raising Your Food-Allergic Child by Marianne S. Barber This book came into my life at the same time as our new Allergy Doctor, Dr. Maryanne Bartoszel Scott, who is listed as a co-writer of the book. I highly recommend this clear and complete book on food allergies. The book is chock full of guidance and information. I WISH I HAD THIS GUIDE WHEN EVAN WAS FIRST DIAGNOSED! It covers the basics such as tips to organize your pantry, ideas on how to handle Halloween, a detailed nutrient and ingredient lists, and even a discussion about marital tension. She also includes some great recipes. It is a "must have!"

Moosewood Cookbook by Mollie Katzen, 1992 edition This cookbook has always been one of my favorites. Katzen includes many egg-free and dairy -free or -optional recipes. I really enjoy vegetarian dishes and am working on getting my kids to love them too, albeit slowly.

The internet is a wonderful tool for parents of children with food allergies. I have compiled an incredible list of valuable links on my LINKS page on my website. Please visit and connect to good support, information, recipes, and help:

www.dairyfreeeggfreekidpleasingcookbook.com

9) **WARNINGS**

Always check the ingredients label EVERY time. Ingredients can and do change. Just recently, TWO of our stand by, reliable foods suddenly included warnings about being processed on equipment with peanuts. Thank goodness there was not an allergic reaction.

Also--don't forget to check your VITAMINS ingredients label--I have noticed several that have dairy protein.

Don't forget that cat and dog food (and corresponding pet treats!) often have dairy and egg ingredients. Move the pet food so it is completely inaccessible to your child and don't let them give the animals any treats that are dangerous.

Organic does not mean "pure." Often organic foods include nut, dairy and/or egg proteins in their ingredients too.

Be watchful about prepared broths—often they include egg and/or dairy proteins. Better yet, always prepare your own with "safe" bouillon.

Beware of soy ice creams! They are often made on equipment with dairy and/or nuts.

I have discovered that sorbets and whole-fruit Popsicles are run on the same lines as regular ice cream and ice cream bars, so beware of both dairy and nut contamination. I have concluded that purchased frozen concoctions are just too risky. I make the homemade variety of Popsicles, and honestly the kids love them just as much.

Remember that dairy, egg, tree-nut, and peanut proteins pass through breast milk. If your child has a severe food allergy, you too must avoid all offending allergen proteins.
Continued:

Your child exhibits a propensity to food allergies. Therefore he or she could develop an allergy to tree nuts and/or peanuts as well (if they are not already diagnosed with one or both). You should scrutinize ingredient lists for these proteins as well and avoid all chance of ingestion.

Note: water chestnuts are actually a legume and coconuts are actually technically a fruit. A person allergic to tree nuts can safely ingest both.

Beware that the MMR vaccine, routinely given to children on their one-year check-up doctor's visit, is developed using egg protein. Avoid a reaction by delaying this vaccination until your child (hopefully and most likely) outgrows his or her egg allergy.

Be aware that flour is sometimes made in factories where other nut flours are also processed, such as almond flour. Call the company and make sure that you are baking with "safe" ingredients. I use Gold Medal's unbleached, all-purpose flour and Stone-Buhr's whole-wheat flour.

Avoid buying bulk foods. Bulk food processing lines are used for all of the bulk food items, including the nut granolas. Treat bulk food items as made on equipment with nuts.

Purchase packaged deli meats for optimum safety. As a former Deli counter service person, I can tell you that at times the slicer is not thoroughly cleaned between cuts of cheese and meat. Treat deli-counter meat as processed on equipment with dairy.

10) LABELING AND CONTACT INFORMATION

Be sure to really think about food product lines. Labeling is not up to full speed yet and while many companies are voluntarily including the "made on equipment with nuts" warning, this is not a legal requirement (yet!). At this point in time, consumers must anticipate products that could be made on shared equipment with nuts (such as bread and ice cream/sorbet) and avoid them. It is a given that store bakeries share all of the equipment and so those delicious walnut brownies and peanut butter cookies that they make do contaminate the bowls and baking trays. Treat all store baking products as "made on equipment with nuts and dairy."

Don't hesitate to track down and call a company and ask them about ingredient information or equipment practices. This can be a frustrating experience, as some companies are seemingly impossible to contact. Be patient and put on your research hats! Use Internet sites as a starting point; often the company states their direct phone number somewhere in the "Contact Us" section. As of October, 2006 the following manufacturers offer the following contact information:

General Mills	(800)328-1144
Kraft	(800)847-1997
Pepperidge Farms	(888)737-7374
Nabisco	(800)622-4726
Frito-Lay	(800)352-4477
Wonder Bread	(800)761-5502
Fantastic Foods	(800)288-1089
Sun Luck	(206)624-4011

11) PARTY PLANNING

I love planning birthday parties and wholly believe that they should be home affairs anyway. I fill the house with safe treats (lollipops and an unregulated potato chip bowl are our favorites), decorations, games, homemade piñata with safe candy, pop, and a big, tailored cake. Thank goodness my husband is a part-time artist and is a whiz with the cake icing. We have successfully created the following themed birthday cakes: Thomas the Tank Engine on a big round cake, R2-D2 on a sheet cake, Bionicle figures on a large frosted sheet cake, a "Scout Walker" figure from **Continued**:

Star Wars out of a few sheet cakes with some carving and icing detail, as well as a snake-shaped cake, a great rocket-shaped cake, and a pirate ship made out of layered, frosted cake sheet sections with homemade apple leather sails. See Family Fun Magazine's website (www.familyfun.com) for other birthday party suggestions, ideas and inspiration.

For a tailored, shaped cake, figure out a good (and "doable") shape. Prepare a couple of sheet cakes from a recipe (see Easy Chocolate Cake in the Dessert section), taking care to ensure equal thickness. Cool completely. Prepare a big cardboard cake platter by folding some foil on a large piece of cardboard. Lay down wax or parchment paper around the outer edges of the cake. Cut out shape(s) and assemble on the paper on the platter. Prepare a thin frosting. Use this frosting to glue the various pieces together and to frost a "crumb layer." Let harden. Prepare a regular consistency frosting and frost the cake completely. Add detail using frosting and a tip. Finally, remove the wax paper from around the sides, removing the accompanying, inevitable mess.

Serve slices of birthday cake with safe soy ice cream (recipe in Desserts section) or without ice cream (with no apologies!).

Prepare a yummy fruit punch using Sprite or 7-Up pop, with frozen balls of fruit juice (use your ice tray).

Plan some fun games and give them "safe" candy for prizes.

Relive your childhood and purchase or make your own piñatas! Fill them with allowable candy and be the star of the party. We made the best "TIE Fighter" piñata for our son's Star Wars themed party. We Paper Mached a balloon with toilet paper rolls attached on either side to cardboard cutout wings. Then we painted the whole thing gray, and then later added great detail with black acrylic paint. (TIP: don't go too crazy with the Paper Mache, or else the kids won't be able to break through the tough layer.).

Love your birthday child up and down and enjoy the fun with the whole invited gang!

12) WEIGHT GAIN IDEAS

I have some ideas to encourage weight gain in your young children. Purchase and use the soymilk "plus" versions. I know that WestSoy and Pacific Soy both have "plus" versions. Make every calorie count. Instead of crackers for snack, offer meat "worms," or fortified cereal, or add big smears of soy nut butter or soy cream cheese on the crackers. Instead of serving your child juice--make fruit smoothies, using soy yogurt, bananas and "plus" soymilk. Freeze any leftover food--perhaps in individual. portions (use small Ziploc bags within a large gallon freezer bag)—to offer a quick reheat for snack time, etc. We usually have two lunches (early and late)--in response to my boys being hungry---if I call it lunch, I prepare something worthy/hearty for maximum nutrition and they are happy with "real" food instead of a lighter snack. Add soy cream cheese and/or vegan cheese to sandwiches, etc. Add mashed tofu to all foods you can think of--tofu really has no taste—so you can "hide" it in many foods and it has great nutritional value. You could add it to any main dish sauce, snack breads or muffins, etc. Use the buttermilk substitute that I have in the substitute section of the book at every opportunity, for instance when a baking recipe calls for regular soymilk.

If you try these tips and your child still doesn't seem to gaining weight, please see your doctor and/or allergist as soon as possible. He/she may have some additional ideas and can also give you a referral to see a nutritionist or dietician. I recommend you see a dietician or nutritionist. Your insurance company should pay for it as well. Feeding children is hard enough without the additional factor of food allergies and mothers can use all of the advice and help that they can get. I wish you success in feeding your vulnerable child!

13) WEBSITE INFORMATION

Visit my website for updates and to peruse links to great resources on the LINKS page of my website:

www.dairyfreeeggfreekidpleasingcookbook.com

Share the site with other mothers needing support. We are all in this together!

14) **SCHOOL**   Along came the day when Evan insisted upon a school experience. He was not to be denied preschool. I was very protective of my sweet, vulnerable boy, but I also wanted him to be "normal," alive, and independent. So I researched all of the local preschools until one met my safety requirements and quality demands.

I searched and found an excellent preschool that was familiar with food allergies, was trained yearly in the use of an epi-pen (the teacher was very on top of this before she met us), was affiliated with the National Association for the Education of Young Children, and allowed only prepackaged snacks with clear labeling. They were receptive to my worries and very welcoming to my child. I prepared a "Snack letter" at the beginning of the year, with a list with all possible dairy-free and nut-free snack options (Evan had outgrown his egg allergy by then). I also kept "Safe" snacks in the cupboard in case Evan couldn't have the snack brought in for the day. I scrutinized the ingredient lists on the snacks every single morning. He thrived at that wonderful preschool and I was so happy to find somewhere I felt comfortable leaving him.

Evan is now in first grade and I am navigating the public school maze. It is LAW: Public schools are mandated to provide a SAFE environment for every student with a disability. A child with a life threatening food allergy is considered to have a disability at school. Schools are mandated to provide a SAFE LUNCH for such students. I am only asking for a safe lunch table and classroom for my food allergic child—I am not asking for a safe lunch to be provided. Therefore—I am not asking too much of my principal and school and nurse to ensure a safe environment for my child!

School policies are usually in place to deal with food allergies that state: "Keep the students safe." But every school district interprets that statement differently AND roles are not clearly defined. The Spokane School District (WA) has a very detailed policy that clearly spells out each district employee's role. That policy is available online and is a great example. This detailed policy was created and enacted after a peanut allergy death on a field trip. By law the state cannot mandate a "Peanut-free" school—because then you'd have to be "free" of everything that could be a problem for students, such as strawberries, dairy, etc. Schools must provide lunch—so you can't remove food from schools.

Food allergic students should not eat the school lunches. Recently two anaphylaxis reactions occurred in schools on the same day, as a result of the food service provider changing distributors of the chicken nuggets without notifying the schools and food allergic kids. There are too many things that can go wrong (contamination, etc) with school lunches!

Schools are more focused on their response to an event and not as focused on the pro-active part of avoiding the accident in the first place. It is up to us parents to gently educate and promote good healthy food policies. We have filled out the 504 plan. This form spells out the medical response plan and legal seriousness of the situation. I passed out a Contact Letter (with a picture) at the beginning of the year to his teacher, lunch ladies, playground duties, and secretaries. I listed the symptoms that would occur if Evan came into contact with dairy and also what it would look like if he ingested dairy. Contact letters should be available in Spanish as well. Snack wasn't an option in half-day Kindergarten, but it is in First Grade. Messy snacks are confined to one table and hands and table are wiped down afterwards, with wipes that I provide. There have been no problems so far. I am unable to persuade the teacher to discontinue snack time.

My son's school does not have a peanut free table in the cafeteria. The tables have "two-seater" benches and Evan sits on one alone, to distance himself from spraying yogurt tubes. I have trained him to eat completely over his lunchbox and to leave anything if it falls on the table or floor and thus becomes contaminated.

Ultimately, our children ARE the last line of defense against a reaction to food allergies. We have to thoroughly train our children about avoiding allergens and what do to if there is contact. Evan is well trained and knowledgeable about his food allergy, but he is still a six-year-old boy. I make sure that all school personnel are prepared in case there is accidental ingestion. I do not want an immature mistake to be a fatal mistake. Evan is a happy, rough and tumble, charismatic school boy who just happens to have a serious food allergy. He is asserting his independence now, unfurling his closely cropped wings.

FINAL THOUGHTS

I am here to tell you that our life without dairy, eggs, or nuts feels perfectly normal now. I have been closely watching my six-year-old son almost every minute of his life: foregoing restaurants, cooking ALL of the time, avoiding most convenience foods, and being very selective about where we go and what we do. It has been a lot of extra work and incredibly stressful. But I have made it through this time and so can you! Just remember--most likely your child will outgrow the food allergies, so this time is fleeting as all precious time with our youngsters is. Diligence is the key ingredient for these years and will pay off in our child outgrowing the allergies.

Do not let the overwhelming daily tasks and stress keep you from enjoying your time with your son or daughter. You did not cause his or her allergy and they did not bring it upon themselves. It is what it is and we can make the best of it. Enjoy your lemonade from the "lemons" that you were dealt! Imagine looking back at this challenging time when he/she is a teenager and realize that you two made it through something difficult together. Who knows? Perhaps this experience can be used as a mental tool when we face the challenge of getting through their adolescence.

Our little ones know nothing about how life "should" be. They do not know they are missing out on ice-cream cones; they just know how lucky and loved they feel when we all go out for lollipops. And really--parenthood is not about what food we give to feed our children's hunger; it is about the love we give to feed their souls.